ALSO BY

Chip R. Bell

MANAGERS AS MENTORS
Building Partnerships for Learning

CUSTOMERS AS PARTNERS
Building Relationships That Last

INFLUENCING
Marketing the Ideas That Matter

Chip R. Bell and Ron Zemke

MANAGING KNOCK YOUR SOCKS OFF SERVICE

SERVICE WISDOM
Creating and Maintaining the Customer Service Edge

Chip R. Bell and Fredric Margolis

UNDERSTANDING TRAINING
Perspectives and Practices

INSTRUCTING FOR RESULTS

Chip R. Bell, Ray Bard, Leslie Stephen, and Linda Webster

THE TRAINER'S PROFESSIONAL DEVELOPMENT HANDBOOK

Chip R. Bell and Leonard Nadler

CLIENTS AND CONSULTANTS
Meeting and Exceeding Expectations

THE CLIENT-CONSULTANT HANDBOOK

DANCE LESSONS

SIX STEPS TO GREAT PARTNERSHIPS IN BUSINESS & LIFE

Chip R. Bell
Heather Shea

Foreword by Tom Peters

Berrett-Koehler Publishers, Inc.
San Francisco

Berrett-Koehler Publishers, Inc.
450 Sansome Street, Suite 1200
San Francisco, CA 94111-3320
Tel: (415) 288-0260 Fax: (415) 362-2512 www.bkpub.com

ORDERING INFORMATION

Individual sales. Berrett-Koehler publications are available through most bookstores. They can also be ordered direct from Berrett-Koehler at the address above.

Quantity sales. Special discounts are available for quantity purchases by corporations, associations, and others. For details, contact the "Special Sales Department" at the Berrett-Koehler address above.

Orders for college textbook/course adoption use. Please contact Berrett-Koehler at the address above.

Orders by U.S. trade bookstores and wholesalers. Please contact Publishers Group West, 1700 Fourth Street, Berkeley, CA 94710. Tel: (510) 528-1444; Fax: (510) 528-3444.

Printed in the United States of America

Printed on acid-free and recycled paper that is composed of 85% recovered fiber, including 15% post consumer waste.

Library of Congress Cataloging-in-Publication Data

Bell, Chip R.
Dance lessons : six steps to great partnerships in business and life / Chip R. Bell, Heather Shea : foreword by Tom Peters.
p. cm.
Includes bibliographical references and index.
ISBN 1-57675-043-4 (alk. paper)
1. Partnership. I. Shea, Heather. II. Title.
HD69.S88453 1998
650.1'3—dc21 98-27938

A **STEPHEN★PUSTEJOVSKY Book** Austin, Texas

Executive editor: Leslie Stephen • Art direction/text and jacket design: Suzanne Pustejovsky
Copyediting: Jeff Morris • Proofreading: Deborah Costenbader and Jamie Fuller • Index: Joanne E. Clendenen
Composition/production: Round Rock Graphics • Cover photo: Cheryl Maeder/FPG International LLC
Step One photo: Mark Scott/FPG International LLC; Step Two Photo: SuperStock Inc.; Step Three photo: Telegraph Colour Library/FPG International LLC; Step Four photo: Cheryl Maeder/FPG International LLC; Step Five photo: Patti Bose Photographics, Orlando, FL; and Step Six photo: Patti Bose Photographics, Orlando, FL.

First Edition 04 03 02 01 00 99 98 10 9 8 7 6 5 4 3 2 1

DEDICATED TO

Nancy Rainey Bell

and

Yvonne Luke Gubner

CONTENTS

STEP FOUR

STEP FIVE

STEP SIX

FOREWORD

by Tom Peters

You don't have to be a good dancer to be a good partner. Fact is, you don't have to know how to dance at all . . . except metaphorically speaking.

I've often said that I'm nuts about a good metaphor. Because in these traumatic, wild and woolly, topsy-turvy times, this age of brainware, creativity, paradox, unreason . . . pick your favorite expression . . . unforgettable word-pictures are our most practical guides, our real-life strategic plans for thriving in this chaos. And Chip Bell and Heather Shea have a vision of partnership that's exactly right for these turbulent times. Just like modern jazz or theater . . . or some of our well-worn sports analogies . . . dancing gives us a fast and lasting image of how the BIW (best-in-world) partnerships work.

And who needs this partnership-as-a-dance stuff? Everybody, and I mean E-V-E-R-Y-B-O-D-Y. Unless you've been out of this world for the last 10 or 15 years, you know that we've said bye-bye to organizations-as-we've-known-them-for-the-last-250 (or so)-years. You know that the most successful "organizations" today are ever-shifting, temporary—or, at most, semi-permanent—strategic alliances, formed to exploit some (probably fleeting) opportunity in the marketplace.

Think about any great dance partnership . . . Rogers and Astaire, Kelly and O'Connor, Fonteyn and Nureyev . . . what's going on there? what went into those standing-ovation results? Years of hard work, practice, basic training . . . well, sure. Plus originality, personal chemistry, everlasting experimentation, constant innovation, trust . . . even more important. Oh, yeah . . . and passion.

BIW strategic alliances are just like that . . . a special blending of brain and muscle, heart and soul, passion and persistence that come from the PEOPLE in the relationship. Doesn't matter whether we're talking about Motorola's global supplier-producer relations or the next project you're doing with those folks down the hall. Commitment, compatibility, information sharing, a passion for precision execution, trust . . . all that soft stuff . . . that's what makes those partnerships great. And . . . I've said this over and over, and I'll say it again . . . there's no excuse for not being great.

So, no need to trot the leg-warmers out of mothballs. Just fire up the synapses that spark IMAGINATION and INNOVATION in your brain, and get ready for a real workout. This stuff takes (lots of) effort . . . but it's worth it—just think about your marriage or your closest friendships.

BIW partners *themselves*—with one another and with countless others (including yours truly at one time or another)—Chip and Heather really know the score about how to make and keep a partnership GREAT.

And . . . I'll say it one more time . . . there's no excuse for not being great. Do what they say, and your next partnership will be.

Tom Peters

July 1998 *Palo Alto, California*

PREFACE

> ***"I think the reason dance has held such an ageless magic for the world is that it has been the symbol of the performance of living."***
>
> **—Martha Graham**

Listen to the sounds of partnership played out on two very different stages.

Setting: The Dance Stage
"We merged at some point . . . like we were one! The first few steps were a bit shaky, we thought later. The audience probably never noticed. We sure did! But at some point when the orchestra seemed to hit its stride, we were there. We were hot. It was pure, totally pure."

Setting: The Conference Room
"We seemed to really click! We've found some terrific synergy. To be frank, it was touch and go right out of the starting block. But once we were up to full speed on our first joint project, we found the groove quickly. Everything fell into place. It's been a success on all sides."

The ability to develop and maintain productive partnerships is *the* critical success factor in today's world. Yet it is the art, not the science, of a partnership that determines its success. Whether that collective enterprise is a powerful corporate alliance, an award-winning dance team, or a loving marriage, the true artists of partnering know it is the heart and soul of the alliance that keep it going despite occasional missteps and setbacks.

No art form more easily captures what goes on in a great partnership than dance. When we think musician, sculptor, or painter, "solo" races to the front of our mind. But mention partnership as a dance and we instantly "get" the imagery; the analogy is clear and compelling. Partnership is a dance—one that can make your feet sore while it lets your heart soar!

This book is about making partnerships *great*—not just satisfactory, not just adequate, not just okay. If you picked this book up hoping to learn about the methods and mechanics of structuring corporate alliances, please put it back and select another. If you got here hoping for a pragmatic primer on the legal, financial, or technical components of the coalitions of commerce, you will probably be disappointed. All those ingredients—legal and financial, technical and mechanical—are important. However, they all hang by strings attached to the heart and soul of the union.

This book is also about making *everyday* partnerships great. We talk far more about partnerships having to do with the cubicle across the aisle, the department down the hall, or the merchant down the street—*everyday partnerships*—than those global, mega–strategic alliances crafted in boardrooms or ornate offices on mahogany row. We are thinking of the key vendor with whom you need a deeper bond, the important customer with whom you seek a mutual covenant, or a valued friendship that is ready for a richer union. Partnerships are everywhere, every way and every day. Many are in despair, some are fair, and great ones are rare. This book is the treasure map for your pursuit of high-quality alliances.

We promise a robust review of what makes partnering a powerful and exhilarating dance. In our research on partnership success, we interviewed a wide range of people currently participating in great partnerships. The metaphor of dance enabled us—and them!—not only to gain fresh perspectives on what makes partnerships work well but also to tap an unconventional source of insight and inspiration.

We are hopeful that as you read this book you will learn a lot about great partnerships and maybe even a little about great dancing! We are confident you will gain useful information and fresh insights on how to

- decide if partnership is *right for you,*
- select the *right form* of partnership,
- *get ready* to partner,
- *pick* good partners,
- *practice* effective partnering,
- deal with *difficult* partners and partnerships,
- know when the partnership is *ready to end,*
- *manage* the factors that lead to partnership greatness, and
- keep *learning* about great partnering.

Partnerships are becoming more important and more complex as the driving coalitions of commerce. Organizations and units seek to partner with vendors, unions, competitors, and customers. Outsourcing ancillary functions produces special opportunities best capitalized on with partnership tools. Teams succeed because of interpersonal forming-storming-norming-performing abilities, not because of talent, tactics, or strategy. Successful teams, units, and organizations are dropping hierarchical, authority-driven structures in favor of nimble confederations better suited for the rapid and agile mobilization of talent. All these alliances rise and fall based far less on the soundness of their settlements and far more on the success of their synergy.

Partnering is on the rise. But "partnership" can mean many things. It can imply the temporariness of the person sitting across the bridge table or the longevity of the person lying beside you in a marriage. The relationship can be as intense as the one you have with your associate in a boardroom and as friendly as the target of your "Howdy!" in a Texas barroom.

There are likewise multiple prescriptions for partnership success. One absolute is this: partnerships are far too complicated for easy instructions. With that in mind, we offer both "stage directions" and an early warning. Our directions on partnership greatness are not presented as lockstep rules; our fourteen lessons were constructed with the idea that you would need to do a fair amount of "adjust to fit." Our early warning is this: it isn't the stage manager's great directions that have the audience shouting "Encore!" after a great finale, so don't get so wrapped up in our instructions that you forget to use your own head and heart.

Partnerships are forever becoming and never complete. Like great dances, great partnerships are never perfect—there is always another lesson to be learned, another routine to be practiced. As dancer and choreographer Gene Columbus says, "A dance is a pursuit. You never call yourself the best because you are always striving to be better." Solid partnerships will continually heed their own special version of ". . . five, six, seven, eight!" They know that, at some level, rehearsals never end. This is the manual for that perpetual pursuit of mastery.

We want you to get the absolute most from this book. We hope you will want to read all the words rather than just scan some of them. *Dance Lessons* was assembled like a dancer's notebook. There are the formal lessons—the instructions and directions—to be sure, but you will also see tips and quips, models and metaphors drawn from our imaginations and from very real stories in the world of business and the world of dance. Together they make a complete picture of partnership greatness. If you examine only certain parts, you may draw incomplete conclusions. While you are obviously free to read what you like, we encourage you to read all the pieces, in sequence.

Make these "dance lessons" come alive! Reading this book without thinking about how it applies to your situation denies you the pragmatism we intend and the practical support you may need. Before reading the book, identify a relationship you seek to develop into a partnership, an alliance you wish to improve, a skill you want to enhance, or a partnership problem you want to solve. While you read, make notes on how you might apply the techniques you find. Another approach might be to make this book the text for a review of an existing partnership. Each of you might read a section independently and then meet to explore its implications for your partnership.

Share this book with all your "dance partners"—your colleagues, associates, vendors, customers, suppliers, stakeholders. This book doesn't contain secrets aimed at making you look good to an unwitting partner. The more you know about how to partner, the more likely all your relationships will be great. The same is true for your partners.

We hope you enjoy *Dance Lessons*! And we would like your feedback on its usefulness as well as your ideas on ways it might be improved in future editions. You will find our address at the bottom of the last page of the book. Drop us a line, fax, or email note, or give us a call. In the meantime, break a leg!

July 1998

Chip R. Bell
Dallas, Texas

Heather Shea
Orlando, Florida

THANKS

Few activities are more interdependent than writing a book. While the image of a recluse writer pounding a keyboard is the "author picture" in most people's heads, a published book reflects the collective efforts of many. These are the pages we use to say "thank you" to the many people who joined us in this demanding but jubilant dance.

Three teams worked with us on *Dance Lessons*. The Texas production team was headed by Leslie Stephen in Austin. The look of the book was crafted by an extraordinarily creative art director, Suzanne Pustejovsky. World-class editor Jeff Morris fashioned the sound of the book. And Leslie delivered a stunning performance as leader, coach, cheerleader, worrier, fixer, and inspirer in her nonstop commitment to making this book a showstopper.

The California publishing team was led by Steve Piersanti, president of Berrett-Koehler Publishers, whose entire staff reflects a commitment to great partnerships in business and life. With marketing director Pat Anderson and production director Elizabeth Swenson, Steve remained steadfast in the quest to facilitate depth, meaning, and significance from a book that began as a random collection of note cards!

The crack research and business-and-life team of Debbie and Cliff Dickinson in Orlando put in yeoman effort doing countless hours of partner interviews. They helped us discover important learnings from their reams of transcripts. We are also grateful to the people who reviewed early drafts of the manuscript and gave us valuable feedback for sharpening it up: Chris Clarke-Epstein, Gabriela Melano, Randy Kosinski, and Victoria Spoor.

We also give a special thanks for the great insights we got from choreographer Gene Columbus, manager of entertainment staffing at Walt Disney World Entertainment.

The coaching of Chip's business partners, Ron Zemke and Tom Connellan of Performance Research Associates, helped bring real-life relevance to the book. The music of Larry Gatlin and The Gaithers (Bill, Gloria, and friends) provided inspirational connection to the muses during the writing process. A world of thanks from Heather to Tom Peters and Ben Vereen for believing in her and encouraging her to live her dream and to David Mulvey and Elaine Burns for caring for her and the next generation of dancers. We are especially grateful to Valerie Oberle for her work with Heather that sparked the original idea for the book, and we are indebted to our family, friends, colleagues, and clients for the countless lessons we have learned from them over the years about great partnerships.

Finally, this book would not have happened without the emotional support and endless love of our families: Nancy Rainey Bell, Bilijack Bell, Bianca Shea, Portia Shea, Judy Terry, and Richard Gubner.

To all of you . . . a heartfelt thanks.

INTRODUCTION

Shall We Dance?

The conference room was an "auditorium" of pure energy! The leader of a large engineering firm was engrossed in an intense exchange on marketing strategy with the leader of a manufacturing company. Their partnership, now six months old, had taken on a show-stopping synergy neither had expected. Associates from each organization entered and exited as if performing a well-rehearsed script. Yet this latest project was a brand-new joint venture.

Almost completing each others' sentences, the two leaders shifted from thorny discord to affirming harmony. They "danced" their way to resolution, agreement, and commitment. When they concluded their discussion and stood to shake hands, their associates spontaneously broke into loud applause. As if on a real stage, the two turned toward the crowd and jokingly bowed to their fans.

THE WORLD OF ENTERPRISE IS ALREADY TEEMING WITH THE SOUNDS OF partnership. Visit your local bookstore and you may be surprised at the large number of books with "partnership" in their titles or subtitles. Countless organizations tout the concept of "partnering" in their ads or PR pap. Most successful business units and organizations report they have been inundated with requests from others that "we get together and explore how we might form an alliance." Yet far more partnerships fail than succeed.

Those enterprises and entities that succeed do so because they have a clear sense of the requirements for great partnering. Those that bring the house down at curtain call are those that never stop rehearsing, even after a stream of great reviews and standing ovations. They have to dance, they know how to dance, they keep "taking lessons" to perpetually stay at the top of their dance . . . and they love to dance. Partnership is the dance of the new millennium.

"Partnership is not the paperwork, it is the human dimension."

—Pat Heim, author of *Hardball for Women*

Partnership: The Work Version of Marriage

We define "partnership" as "*a deliberate blending of capacities for the continuous mutual benefit of involved parties.*"

Let's look at the key parts of that definition. First, partnerships must be "continuous" . . . they dance until the music stops. This means that partnerships have a momentum; each encounter has a tie back to the last. Some partnerships have only a few encounters; some go on for many years. We do not assume partnerships must have a "forever" intention to qualify—that's a marriage. On the flip side, if the relationship is likely to be a single encounter it fails to qualify. Single-encounter relationships are transactions—like the mechanic at the repair shop, the receptionist at the dentist—a solitary shuffle-hop-step. We generally want such transactions to be agile, able, and amiable, not intimate, intense, and interdependent.

Partnerships are *"a blending of capacities."* "Blend" implies a mixture, not necessarily equal parts. It also implies a kind of worked-out amalgamation of shared assets. "Capacities" is our word for the array of "stuff" that partners might bring to the relationship. That stuff could be information, good will, capital, or other resources.

"Partnership is like intertwining threads . . . together they make a rope."

—Louise Lague, The Wisdom Group

"Mutual benefit" means that all parts of the partnership must derive adequate gain from the relationship. While reciprocity is a requirement, perfect balance is a momentary occurrence and not an everlasting prerequisite. Relationships with the benefits all weighted to one side are relationships based on dependence; the one-sidedness in time becomes a parasitic arrangement as the giver gets weaker and more angry, the taker stronger and more selfish. In time, the connection collapses under its own dysfunction.

"Deliberate" and *"involved parties"* both strongly communicate that partnerships entail assertive effort. While we believe partnerships can be formed by accident, we do not believe they can be maintained by accident.

But partnership is more than a word to be defined in a book. "It is a process, not a transaction," Terry McElroy, senior vice president of McLane Company, reminds us. "Partnership is the work version of marriage," says Marcia Corbett, vice president of marketing for AchieveGlobal, "not in the sense of permanence, but certainly in the sense of depth, commitment, and loyalty. It is born out of an honest realization that you have needs and goals you cannot meet or maximize without a partner."

These definitions and descriptions inform us that partnerships are both potent and pervasive. When you invite a colleague to be an ongoing sounding board for your ideas, in exchange for your keeping an eye out for assignments for which she might be qualified, you are partnering. When you offer a key vendor special status with the expectation that he will bring you his best solutions first, you are partnering. When you agree with your significant other that you will do all the housework, feed the "livestock," and wash the car in exchange for pot roast on Friday night, you are partnering (not particularly wisely, in our opinion, but reciprocity is in the eye of the beholder). Partnerships are everywhere, in countless ordinary interpersonal associations. Given how much time we invest in them, when we improve our partnerships, we improve our lives.

"Partnership is the work version of marriage."

—Marcia Corbett, AchieveGlobal

Dance: The Landscape of the Soul

It is said that great dancers learn their steps so they can forget them. They practice to a point they can simply hear the music and move. Great partnerships also reach a point of such intuitive oneness that they can operate with magical harmony and stunning grace. However, as in dance, the path to greatness takes deliberate steps, each practiced with care, commitment, and consistency. *Dance Lessons* is an instruction manual for stepping to greatness.

The wisdom and warnings we share with you in *Dance Lessons* came through in-depth interviews with a wide range of people highly experienced in great partnerships. Their organizations were as mainstream as Marriott, as niche as USAA, and as avant-garde as the Broker Restaurants. Some were well known, like the Disney Institute; some were new partnerships, like AchieveGlobal, an alliance originally made up of three famous training companies.

Our interviews predictably confirmed much we already knew. Great partnerships are populated by partners who conduct their selection process very carefully. They have clear goals and worked-out-in-advance cues. They take the time to explore how they plan to end the dance before they take to the floor. They are relationships that exhibit as much passion as discipline; they are as emotional as they are rational.

Our interviews also gave us some unanticipated insights. We discovered that the steps toward greatness are precise and consistent. So, using dance as our metaphor, we constructed our text around the six steps we heard described repeatedly in our interviews. We also learned that great partnerships spend far, far more time getting ready to partner than we expected. For that reason, the partnership itself—we call it "dancing"—doesn't begin until our Step Four! Steps One through Three all focus on getting ready for the main event.

One additional unexpected discovery. Great partners all talk about having the same core commitments—we call them protocols. A protocol is a no-need-to-explain kind of routine that partners accept, value, and depend on. Chess players don't have to decide on the moves a pawn is allowed; football players don't argue over how many points a touchdown is worth. While our interviewees used vastly different words to describe what goes on in a great partnership, we found the same protocols operating in all of them.

We learned that great partnerships begin their relationship *expecting the best* from it. This standard not only serves as a criterion for achievement, it provides a noticeable self-fulfilling optimism. Partners work diligently to always *assert the truth*. This proactive gesture keeps integrity at the forefront of all their dealings. Consistent with this value is a focus on perpetually *keeping agreements*, ensuring that the partnership is filled with trust and commitment.

Great partners are always quick to *honor their partner*. By lacing the relationship with deep respect and noticeable admi-

"Partnership may be a legal term, but it is fundamentally not a legal concept. Bottom line, it is two or more people serving the relationship by serving each other."

—John Campbell, Brookfield Management Services

ration, the partners achieve more without wasting energy on suspicion. They place enormous emphasis on having passionate connections—we call it *being all, there*—meaning that great partners bring all they have to every encounter. Finally, the resilience and allegiance they bring to their collective mission form a protocol we label *stay . . . on purpose.*

"Dance is the landscape of the soul."

—Martha Graham

While we will explore these protocols in depth in Step Three: Rehearsing, we refer to them throughout the book as the underpinnings of each step to partnership greatness.

Six Steps to Greatness

Our concept of a partnership dance has six steps for success: *Focusing, Auditioning, Rehearsing, Dancing, Hurting,* and *Bowing Out.* Within each step are two or three lessons. The lessons detail the basic choreography of partnership as well as offer various "bite-size" tips and techniques for your review, reflection, and practice. To help you zero in on how to use what is to come, here is a brief description of the objective of each step.

Step One. Focusing: Preparing to Partner

Dancing is a method of expressing a much deeper purpose than the mere movement of feet and limbs, torso and head. Great dancers would be great painters if their talents lay in that direction. It is the intense focus on excellent creative expression that fuels the dancer, not the dance itself. As relationship dances, partnerships must be grounded in a clear commitment to some purpose that can best be expressed through a partnership. Partners who partner for partnering's sake stop dancing long before the music stops. Before choosing your "footwork," you must focus deep inside to find the common purpose that will inspire you to partnership greatness.

Step Two.
Auditioning: Picking Great Partners

As an early test to ensure good partnership fit, auditions are all about discovery and disclosure. They are the method great partnerships use not only to identify their special talents, but also to create a setting for learning and communicating expectations. This step will delve into an assortment of "starting" issues important to choosing the right partner; it will also tell you how to craft the cues that can offer an early warning to postpone or cancel the dance before your investment in the partnership makes "calling it curtains" awkward.

Step Three.
Rehearsing: Getting the Partnership in Shape

Most masters of partnerships warn that the early stages of a relationship are the most critical. Choreographing the relationship involves identifying all the important first steps and walking through them deliberately, shutting out any distractions. Naysayers speak loudest in the opening scenes, when the partnership is most vulnerable given the newness of the dance. Your early focus should be on "working the plan," ignoring any opposition or objections. Great dancers use rehearsal time to focus on their feet and dance the steps. This section will offer tips for effective "foot watching."

> ***"Partnerships are hard work. It's not occasional cigars and cognac . . . it is working hard at it—all the time."***
>
> **—Michael Metzler, Metzler & Company**

Step Four.
Dancing: Keeping the Magic in Motion

Step Four is all about finding and keeping the feel or flow of the dance. Hear the message here: dancing is our fourth step, not the first. Preparation is paramount for great performances. Partnerships are greatness in the making. They are hopeful pursuits of magic, not efforts valued only at the finale. While there is no sure-fire, secret formula for everlasting partnership progress, we describe the many ways great partnerships consciously keep going and growing.

Step Five.
Hurting: Managing the Pain in Partnership

Great dances are rarely forever flawless. Muscles ache, costumes fray, stagehands tire, and dancers complain of having an off night. Mature dancers manage their misery and bounce back to star again. Their long-term resilience rests in their capacity to bend against anguish and continue to dance even in adversity; they know pain is more a teacher than torturer, a mentor for mastery rather than an agent of agony. This section describes several common partnership pains and provides remedies for either avoiding them or weathering their presence.

Step Six.
Bowing Out: Calling It Curtains

Our research on partnership revealed a special discovery: endings can be as important as beginnings. Partnerships sometimes deteriorate into animosity because the partners are unable to recognize “ending” signals and dance on after the music has stopped. The ill-timed finish leaves the partners angry, bitter, and reluctant to dance again. The lessons in this section are anchored in the belief that a purposeful adjournment is as vital to partnership greatness as a purposeful audition.

Partnerships aren’t for everyone, any more than dancing. Great partnerships require an investment of energy much greater than casual relationships or superficial transactions call for. Partnerships are clearly not a cakewalk. They require skipping and jumping—and sweating, lots of sweating. Partnerships also demand vulnerability, a willingness to fall and to get dropped. And partnerships diminish the protection of anonymity; they are poor associations in which to hide. Partnership means working on stage, not backstage. Imperfections and insecurities prance across the performance in full view. Done well, partnerships work at amplifying disclosure and enhancing exposure.

When not founded for the right purpose with the right people, partnerships can also be a dreadful waste of emotional energy. Because of the energy they exact, they are often an unsuitable configuration for collective effort. Far too many partners try to promenade home when cheerful walks down separate paths would have been better. So beware the fad side of partnership. Easy alliances may form in the infatuated glow of "love at first sight." And clearly there are occasional examples of the accidental magical match made in early enraptured moments. But most partnerships are hard won through relevant purpose, careful choosing, cautious courtship, and constant toil.

We can watch *The Gay Divorcee*, *Saturday Night Fever*, *Dirty Dancing*, or *Shall We Dance?* and suddenly get new insights into the poetry of partnership. Scrape away the legalese, the obsession with form, and the cerebral calibration of clever contract clauses, and what is left? A bond of kindred spirits, a union seeking a setting for truth, a context for trust, and a crucible for generosity.

Naked partnership is about soul. And soul is what most makes it akin to dance. Since great partnerships provide a platform for so vast an array of emotions and talents, they truly are landscapes of the soul.

The Legal Side of Partnership

Legally, a partnership is defined as "an association of two or more people to carry on as co-owners a business for profit." While people often use the word "partner" without intending the precise legal relationship, in the eyes of the law, a partnership is a partnership if certain criteria are met. Electing to call your grouping a partnership, or electing to deny that your grouping is a partnership, is not a relevant test regarding whether a partnership legally exists.

We included a bit of legalese since these issues may arise in forging the interpersonal side of your coalition. Before going very far down the partnership route, it might be a good idea to visit your local attorney or the legal department of your organization. Too many well-intentioned alliances are forged without concern for the legal liability of the entangled. And few events can threaten the viability of a trusting partnership more than to have it unexpectedly come under the scrutiny and scalpel of a court of law.

"Aw," you may say, "we're not really a partnership. We're just a(n) . . . (choose one) alliance, association, joint venture, union, confederation." Are you clear on what these terms mean? Are there liability or other legal implications for your choice? Unfortunately, we live in a highly litigious world. Partnerships risk losing unexpectedly high stakes as well as unpredictably getting into great snares if they do not at least review the legal components of the relationship.

There are many forms a partnership can take—limited partnerships, corporations, alliances, associations, joint ventures, unions, or confederations. Each carries a different connotation and legal ramifications. And remember this important point made earlier: electing to call your grouping a partnership, or electing to deny that your grouping is a partnership, is not a relevant test regarding whether a partnership legally exists. Be careful.

Elements of a partnership in the legal sense of the word are that it is: (1) a voluntary association of two or more persons (with or without a written or oral agreement) (2) formed with the intent to carry on (3) as co-owners (exercising joint control) (4) a business for (with the intent of making a) profit. The Uniform Partnership Act, adopted in almost every state, suggests that co-ownership of property, sharing of gross returns, sharing profits are not necessarily prima facie evidence of partnership. The most persuasive components are subjective intent, type of activity (i.e., business), and co-ownership.

There are numerous forms of partnerships under statutory law. Limited partnerships have the same elements as general partnerships except for the element of co-ownership. In limited partnerships there is one general partner, who actively manages the affairs of the business and assumes unlimited liability, and one or more limited partners, who act in a passive role with restricted rights to manage the business and whose liability is limited to the amount of their investment. The main purpose of limited partnerships in the United States has been to create a way for a business enterprise to acquire equity capital without subjecting the investor to the liability that arose from the business operations.

Another form of business association is the corporation, an entity with some of the aspects of a partnership, but which separates ownership and control. Multiple residual claimants (e.g., stockholders) delegate to directors and officers the responsibility of day-to-day operations. Since the owners' capital investments are fungible (i.e., exchangeable), their share in the business can be freely transferable. A variation on the theme is the closely held corporation, in which membership is limited rather than open (as in a publicly held corporation with freely traded shares). Think of a corporation as serving the needs of many members; a partnership serving the needs of a few.

An "alliance" is defined by *Black's Law Dictionary* as a "union for objects of common interest to the contracting parties." *Black's* defines "association" as "the act of a number of persons in uniting together for some special purpose or business. It is a term of vague meaning used to indicate a collection or organization of persons who have joined together for a certain or common object." Eberhard E. Scheuing defines a "joint venture" in his book *The Power of Strategic Partnering* as "two organizations that closely link their fortunes by forming a new legal entity in which they both invest capital (usually fifty-fifty) and which they thus jointly own." A "union" is defined in *Black's* as "an unincorporated association of persons for a common purpose." And a "confederation" is a "league or compact for mutual support."

You can quickly see how muddy the concept can be.

STEP One

"How can we know the dancer from the dance?"

—W. B. Yeats

FOCUSING

Preparing for Partnership

They had come far since deciding to dance together for their big run at the Nationals. Now the compulsory dances were over, and the six finalist couples were each to perform their choice of dance and music for the final judging. They were to be the sixth and last couple . . . and they had chosen to dance the tango to *Hernando's Hideaway*, going against their usual squeaky-clean, boy-and-girl-next-door image to try to coax a national championship from the judges.

As the fifth couple took the floor, they heard the opening strains of *Hernando's Hideaway*. Had they made a mistake in the sound booth? Had somebody gotten the music for the dances mixed up? They

Heels or Flats? Boots or Toe Shoes?

Take a minute to think about a particular partnership of yours. It could be one you are starting up, one you are in now, or one you are considering in the future. Review the descriptions at each end of the ten scales below. On each scale, circle the number that best represents the relationship you have in mind.

I expect our relationship to be intensely interdependent.	5 4 3 2 1	I expect our relationship to be more like a valuable support system.
What we have at stake is pretty much equal.	5 4 3 2 1	What we have at stake is far from the same.
We will march to our own drum, without the approval of others.	5 4 3 2 1	We are very dependent on others to make this partnership work.
The risk of failure is moderate.	5 4 3 2 1	The risk of failure is very high.
We expect this union to last a long time.	5 4 3 2 1	We honestly expect this union to last a relatively short time.
It is our idea.	5 4 3 2 1	It is their idea.
I want to do this project.	5 4 3 2 1	My boss/organization wants to do this project.
We know them and their products/services.	5 4 3 2 1	We don't know them very well.
We need them; they need us.	5 4 3 2 1	We could do this without them.
We are intrigued by their talents.	5 4 3 2 1	They are practical suppliers.

Now, add up the numbers you circled and divide by ten to get your "dance quotient."

If your dance quotient is a:	*Your partnership is a:*
5	Tango
4	Waltz
3	Square Dance
2	Twist
1	Line Dance

watched the fifth couple eagerly start their routine—a tango!—and realized the frightful truth: they would have to perform the exact same dance, to the exact same score.

In their panic, they barely heard the emcee announce, "Our sixth couple has also chosen to dance the tango." As the first few notes of *Hernando's Hideaway* blared again over the speakers, their legs began to feel numb. They stared blankly at one another as they struggled to remember what their first step was supposed to be.

All championship dancers, while waiting their turn before the fickle eyes of a judge, think, "What am I doing here?!" Those who succeed are those who can calm distraction, remember complex steps, and self-talk their way to self-confidence. But these are not the only critical success factors. Choosing to dance the right dance for the right reason sets the stage for successfully displaying the dancers' talent and skill.

DO YOU WANT TO DANCE?

Partnerships come in many forms and are given many labels—alliances, confederations, coalitions, guilds, associations, unions, even friendships and marriages. Dances are similar . . . many forms, many labels. Partnerships can be company to company (as Ford might be to Mazda), unit to unit (as the Operations Group might be to the Sales Division), or unit to company (as the Purchasing Department might be to ABC Office Supplies, Ltd.). The labels don't really matter—one person's alliance is another person's association.

When you are focusing on getting ready to partner, it is more useful to think about a partnership in terms of its purpose. We do not mean "purpose" in the sense of mission or vision, but rather in terms of the function or reason for the partnership. The purpose of the partnership can dictate its duration and depth of involvement as well as signal the potential challenges the partners will face.

Your score from our Heels or Flats? exercise (opposite) will help you focus on what you might expect from your partnership "dance." As you read the following descriptions, pay particular attention to the perils or dangers of the type you are considering.

The Tango

The Tango is our label for the highest level of partnership. In a real tango, the dancers are very different identities (male and female) who symbolically complete each other. They must be able to anticipate and execute intricate footwork while moving almost as one.

Other real dances that share these characteristics to some degree are the rumba, the samba, the quick step, the paso doble, and some forms of ballet—as well as jitterbugs done extremely well. Recall blind Al Pacino and Gabrielle Anwar in *Scent of a Woman*, or Patrick Swayze and Jennifer Grey in *Dirty Dancing*, or the final competition scene of *Strictly Ballroom.* The physical and mental preparation for dancing at this level can be intense.

Tango partnerships are up close and personal. They require intense emotional investments. The partners' values must absolutely blend, not just be reasonably compatible. And the trust requirement is extremely high. Partners in a Tango relationship often characterize it with emotional phrases like "We're joined at the hip," "We're soul mates," or "I don't know where *we* begin and *they* end."

Great Tango partnerships require incredibly intense energy and time, particularly in the beginning. And they are easy targets for such evils as jealousy and possessiveness. Since the trust level is so high, the fall when one partner betrays the other is so far . . . and painful.

Tango partners place more value on loyalty than any of the other partnership types. In fact, they must work hard to avoid blind loyalty. They can be fiercely protective of one another—and their time together—sometimes to the detriment of other relationships important to one or both partners.

Tangos are best suited to partnering opportunities where a very high level of interdependence will be required. Such relationships are common when neither partner can do what the other does and the synergy their association will produce is valued equally by each partner. Tango partnerships are also important when trust around proprietary or highly confidential information is vital to success.

The Tango form is a must for alliances that cannot afford the costs of partnership failure and therefore seek a relationship that is thoroughly interconnected. Another situation that demands a Tango relationship is when the partnership must move as one very quickly, with minimal explanation or discussion.

One of the world's leading distributors of after-market motorcycle and power sports vehicle products is Fort Worth, Texas–based Tucker Rocky Distributing. President Frank Esposito described a Tango partnership of theirs this way:

One of our most financially successful partnerships is with a helmet manufacturer in Taiwan. Our core competency is distribution and market knowledge; theirs is cutting-edge design and manufacturing. We partnered with them to develop a completely new brand of helmet. And we guaranteed a very large number of helmet orders. Our communication is intensely open; trust is complete and without reservations. Today, other distributors knock on their door wanting a piece of their business. They say, "No thanks, we have all we need with our company, Tucker Rocky!"

Partners in Tango relationships must place continual emphasis on renewal and growth. A frequent partnership checkup can be a valuable opportunity to ensure there is a "meeting of the hearts." Ironically, the risk that a Tango partnership will fail is only moderate, since the partners' initial commitment is so high. However, the risk at performance time is also significant—a Tango fall on the stage or in the marketplace can be very painful. On the other hand, the impact of the environment or context on the success of the Tango partnership is low. Tango partnerships are rarely distracted by the audience—they "dance to their own music."

The Waltz

The Waltz is a catchall label for a wide range of everyday ballroom dances—including the Texas two-step, the fox trot, the cha cha, and the polka. The Waltz partnership has some of the characteristics of the "two people melted together" Tango, but with far less emotional investment.

Partners who "waltz" simply enjoy the grace and rhythm of their collective response to the music, as opposed to Tango partners, who hear the beating of their respective hearts. Think of a Waltz partnership as being a Tango that has been tamed by simplifying the steps and dampening the passion of the dance. Obviously, with less emotional investment, the propensity for deep disappointment is far less in a Waltz than in a Tango.

A key peril of a Waltz partnership is the participants may find so much strength in the form of the relationship that they never tap the potential emotional depth of partnering. Waltzers make easy assumptions that Tangos avoid. And, unlike Tango partners who never miss one another's subtle cues, no matter how loud the surrounding noise, Waltzers are easily distracted by peripheral issues. They are quick to look outside the partnership, for example, for quick solutions to problems or for a shot of creative energy.

Waltzes are the right form of partnership when some aspects of the relationship need the security of a well-heeled alliance but other aspects can tolerate more freedom. Waltz partnerships are particularly appropriate when the output of the relationship requires tightly coordinated systems and processes but not much emotional interdependence. For instance, the systems of the intertwined entities must work like a Swiss watch, but success is less dependent on the people in the partnership being emotionally close.

When Heather was director of marketing planning and communication for Arthur Andersen & Co., she was responsible for all advertising for the firm's accounting and consulting services. While successful advertising campaigns depended on her department's creative copy, it also was imperative that their ads comply with regulations governing the public accounting profession.

Heather invited a lead attorney in the firm's legal department to "waltz" with her through her ad campaigns, from concept through production. Heather's campaigns gained credibility and punch; his role in the company changed from "bad cop" to trusted advisor.

The Square Dance

Square Dances are moderation in motion. They require a great deal of coordination, but little emotional intensity—real square dancers even partner with different people as they dance! In the words of dyed-in-the-wool professional square dancers Tom and Princess Newhouse of Gun Barrel, Texas, “While you usually promenade home with your original partner, you sashay, allemande left, and do-si-do out on the floor with lots of others.”

Square Dance partnerships usually have very strict rules and protocols, though, and they can be heavily influenced by outsiders, just as the non-dancing caller in a real square dance choreographs the moves on the floor.

Square Dance partnerships are high-risk alliances because of their hybrid nature. The partners often exhibit an uneasy ambivalence—acting sometimes like Tango partners and sometimes more like they are doing the electric slide or some group folk dance. Consequently, they have to work hard to avoid distractions and stay in focus to keep from sidestepping their alliance.

The Square Dance is the logical choice when the partnership is bound by strict external regimens or rules (such as a those governing the healthcare or securities industries) but the players are free to add their own style or flair to how they partner. Square Dances are valuable when the partners need to periodically involve others outside the partnership, either to enrich the relationship or to enable it to achieve a goal it might not otherwise be able to do. The Square Dance form also serves well when the partnership is to be relatively short in duration, but needs to be precise in executing its game plan.

A good example of the Square Dance style is the manner in which The Tom Peters Group approaches partnership. The Peters organization gets countless queries every year about forming alliances. Some are solid opportunities for synergy, but many are from entities who bring little to the table other than their desire to ride on the company’s name. Sorting the stars from the starstruck requires a rational, logical assessment. While they partner with a few, they are very careful not to alter or dilute the company's reputation or the distinction of its name and brand.

When Heather was president of The Tom Peters Group/Learning Systems, the partnership philosophy worked like this:

> *If we were considering a partnership with another company, we would make sure that it was very clear where we were heading and what each of us was going to get out of the partnership. You have to do it in very deliberate terms, not just "Wow, this is exciting, think of the possibilities." Without the tough, rational part up front, when you finally say, "Okay, now let's get married," everyone suddenly goes, "Whoa, time out! This really is serious!"*

The Twist

There are many twist-like dances: the lindy, swing, Charleston, shag, jive, flamenco, bossa nova—and jitterbugs done poorly! All these dances essentially involve two people dancing separately in front of each other. Some of their moves are somewhat connected, but most of the time they are doing their own thing. We consider Twist partnerships to be the middle ground between the moderate Square Dance and the almost completely independent Line Dance.

Twist partnerships are an appropriate form when the lion's share of the work of the alliance will be done independently, but one consequential part is to be done collectively. Twist partnerships are also a good choice when the appearance of having the relationship is more valuable than its substance. This might occur when the perception that two entities work closely together is important in the marketplace, even if their actual relationship is somewhat casual or perfunctory. This is the classical supplier-vendor relationship, like the local car repair shop that touts its genuine NAPA parts.

A recent example of an ill-advised Twist partnership was a well-known candy company that was introducing a specialty candy and sought to partner with a candy wrapper manufacturer. Enormous energy and expense went into creating a unique chocolate bar to tie into a famous movie-related media event.

Unfortunately, millions were lost because the wrapper supplier was unable to provide enough wrappers to respond to unexpected market demand. Their next introduction of a specialty candy item was more carefully partnered—the candy-maker recognized that its vendor needed to be a partner, not simply a supplier.

The Line Dance

The Line Dance is a catchall term for the slew of dances that are more like emotional support groups on the floor than interdependent couplings. Think of various "herd dances" like the bunny hop, the hully gully, the macarena, or the electric slide. With these forms the dancers are completely independent; they are dancing together only because it is more fun to do it in a group.

Line Dance partnerships offer the advantages of assistance and support without all the emotional entanglement. The relationship is not a symbiotic one, where the partners mesh unique capacities. Instead it is a more fluid pairing, in which the partners pool similar offerings in the belief that joining forces will make their output more productive, their processes more efficient, and their effort more satisfying.

Line Dance partnerships are appropriate when the alliance adds value to a product or service in the minds of their customers but neither of the partners is dependent on its success. For example, if Banana Republic, J. Crew, and Ben & Jerry's were to share the same contract parking lot and valet service for the convenience of their collective customers.

Line Dance partnerships work when the convenience and comfort of an ongoing relationship is preferable to a temporary, transaction-specific encounter. They can also be useful for a single or periodic customer-driven event, like an annual "Taste of the Town" affair in which numerous food-based entities partner to promote their business to the entire community.

Partnership Payoffs and Pitfalls

	TYPE OF PARTNERSHIP				
	Tango	**Waltz**	**Square Dance**	**Twist**	**Line Dance**
SUCCESS FACTORS					
Preparation required for success in partnering	High		Moderate		Low
Degree of risk likely	Moderate		High		Moderate
Impact the environment or context has on success	Low		Moderate		High
Level of trust required for success	Very high		High		Moderate
Issue most likely to undermine success	Dependence		Ambivalence		Independence
Typical length of relationship	Long		Moderate		Short
Most likely blind spot	Growth		Focus		Commitment
Most likely hot spot (issue provoking defensiveness)	Possess-iveness		Distraction		Tenacity
Emotional role model	A great marriage		Casual friendship		A good CPA or dentist
Values match required for success	Carbon copies		Basically the same at core		Compatible
Example in Business	Tucker Rocky & Helmet Mfg.				Acme Mfg. & Wile E. Coyote

A well-known Line Dance partnership is the alliance between Wile E. Coyote and Acme Manufacturing in the Warner Bros. *Roadrunner* cartoon series. Clearly there is no emotional involvement . . . Wile E. never complains, and Acme never offers to refund his money when the Whiz Bang Rocket Skates—or whatever—falter in their promise. Yet their relationship is more than a simple series of sales transactions. Wile E. seems supported by the fact that Acme will continue to create and market a continual stream of "Catch the Roadrunner" contraptions, and Acme presumably appreciates the financial benefits of acting as Wile E.'s sole-source supplier.

PREPARING FOR PARTNERSHIP

Are there more partnership types than the Tango, Waltz, Square Dance, Twist, and Line Dance? Of course. There are probably as many variations as there are partnerships. Every relationship is unique. However, think of the types we have described here as being five different dance routines, each with many twists, turns, and lifts. A part of preparing for partnership is choosing the routine that suits you and your prospective partner's situation.

Our Partnership Payoffs and Pitfalls chart (opposite) summarizes the functions and key characteristics of the different types of partnerships. Use it to reflect on the way your current or prospective partnerships are or the way you want them to be.

A PARTNERSHIP IN ACTION

Cary and Dale first met at an industry association conference. The meeting planner had organized a get-acquainted game at the social that involved telling two truths and a lie—and the two of them chose the same "I sang in a rock group in college" lie. In conversation after the icebreaker, they discovered they had even more in common. Sometime later, they served on the ethics committee of the association. And, over breakfast one morning, they elected to bind their two companies in a partnership for collective buying and marketing.

Cary was the CEO of Stan Dup Enterprises; Dale was the CEO of Sid Downe, Ltd. Both companies were about ten years old, with approximately 200 employees. They were in the same industry, but offered unique products and services and did not directly compete.

Cary was a tennis player; Dale played golf. Cary was trained in marketing; Dale was a CPA, a veteran of several years with a large public accounting firm. Cary made decisions from the heart, tending toward intuitive, shoot-from-the-hip judgments. Dale was more methodical, mulling over information and coming to a decision after long and careful consideration. Both were in their early forties and anxious to grow their companies to a more dominant position in their industry.

Cary and Dale were about to dance a Waltz . . .

Some of the characteristics of their prospective partnership tended more toward the Square Dance than the Tango. The expected amount of preparation and risk associated with their partnership, the impact of the environment on its success, and the probable length of their prospective relationship all were moderate. Interpersonally, they were like casual friends with similar values. But, as would be more expected in the Tango form of partnership, they will face the danger of possessiveness and dependence. And they seem likely to suffer the Tango partners' blind spot: they might get so comfortable with one another that they risk stunting the partnership's growth.

In the pages to follow, we will witness the evolution of Cary and Dale's partnership. As they illustrate the triumphs and tribulations of partnering, we will see them drill and sweat; we will watch them miss cues and stumble; we will see them soar and shine.

LESSON

Choosing the Right Partnership for the Right Reasons

1

PARTNERING IS HOT. AND IT SHOULD BE. WHEN DONE RIGHT, for the right reasons and in the right circumstances, partnering is an effective way for individuals with similar business interests to combine their strengths or for two (or more) organizations to gain a mutual competitive advantage. But it's not always appropriate, and not all kinds of partnerships work for all individuals or businesses.

Just as couples sometimes marry for the wrong reasons, businesses sometimes partner for the wrong purposes. Unwary business leaders, units, and organizations stumble into the pitfalls of partnership when a more conventional path might have been an easier and more direct route to success. Before you decide to take the partnering route, first determine whether it will take you where you want to go.

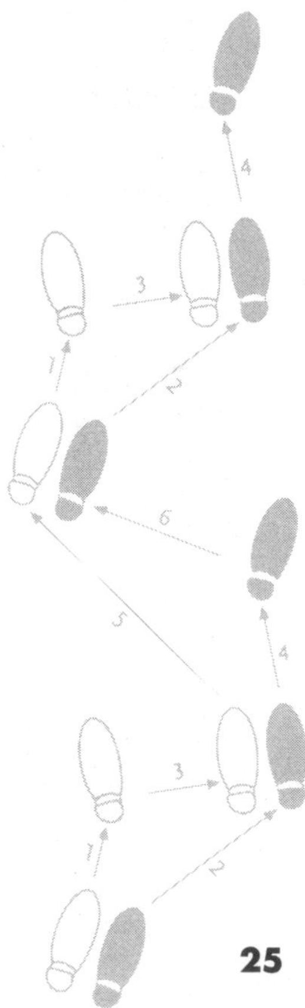

Focus on Form and Fit

There are two main factors to consider when contemplating any partnership arrangement: the overarching purpose of the partnership (What dance shall we dance?) and the personal and commercial compatibility of the partners (With whom shall we dance?). You can pick a dance and a dance partner at random and head toward the bandstand just for the sake of dancing, but you're not likely to gain much satisfaction from such a haphazard enterprise. Instead of gliding across the floor, you'll stumble over each other's feet.

Tapping the Source

Dancing, as Zorba could tell you, is a way of expressing a deep, essential purpose. This is true not only in life but in business as well. The dance of business partnership must be committed to some clear, central purpose that can best be expressed through partnering. All business partnerships, of course, are grounded in some commercial purpose, but they rise to greatness only if a relationship objective is also served.

Dancers know that great dancing begins deep inside—you just "gotta dance." In a business partnership, it's the core purpose that matters, not the process. It's this inner source of creative energy, the clear, common purpose, that gives a partnership the fire and commitment it needs to achieve success—that and being emotionally ready for the rigors of partnering.

Finding a Good Fit

Partners who indulge in partnering for its own sake—because it's "hot"—often find themselves dancing with different partners long before the music stops. When accounting firm Price Waterhouse was considering a merger with competitor Deloitte, Haskins and Sells, the firms' partners in the U.S.

approved the merger with little hesitation. However, the partners in both companies' European offices, where the cultural differences were much greater, axed the deal. Today, Deloitte Touche is the product of a successful merger, but the strains between the dissimilar cultures of Deloitte, Haskins and Sells and Touche Ross still show. Merging their client records and real estate proved far easier than getting this odd couple to dance.

Partnerships succeed when partnership is the right relationship for the partners; they also win because the partners are right for the relationship. The key to making a partnership great is to ensure first that it is grounded on the proper rationale.

"Dance, even when dressed in its richest costumes and most sophisticated techniques, never loses its connection with gut reality."

—F. Borrows, *History of Ballroom Dancing*

Are You Ready for Partnership?

A number of years ago some ministers gave couples contemplating matrimony a pamphlet entitled "Are You Ready to Be Married?" The tract was not about how to make a great marriage; it was a self-evaluation focusing on what it takes to be a good marriage partner. Good business marriages begin with good (but by no means perfect) partners—and partners who want to make it work have certain distinctive characteristics.

The questions in our Self-Test for Focusing are designed to help you look inside yourself to assess whether partnership is the right "dance" for you. They are weighted toward the personal, rather than legal, structural, or economic factors (but remember that in this kind of partnership, "you" includes your organization). If you're already in a partnership, they can be used as a status check—as part of a periodic partnership evaluation to see how you're doing and what needs changing.

A Self-Test for Focusing

- Recall a past relationship that was important to you—one that required effort, energy, and commitment. What did you learn about yourself as a result of this relationship? What would you do differently if you could repeat the relationship?
- What actions will you take if this relationship is never consummated or falters early? What actions will you take if it comes to an unexpected end after you have invested effort, energy, and commitment?
- If this relationships never happens, who will lose? Who will be hurt or embarrassed? What will you expect in return? What will you give up if it never happens?
- For what contribution do you want to be remembered?
- What if your crystal ball told you this relationship would take a greater toll on you than on your potential partner? What would you do differently? What would you say to your potential partner?
- If you think of this partnership as a movie or play, which one comes to mind as the best metaphor? What part would you play? What part would your potential partner play? What does this suggest to you?
- We all want relationships to be fair and reciprocal. No one wants to be the slave in a master-slave relationship, giving almost all and getting little in return. Are you willing for the relationship to be sixty-forty? Seventy-thirty? Eighty-twenty? How would you feel

if you contributed 90 percent and your partner contributed 10 percent? At what point would the imbalance pinch? What does this mean to you?

- If you were the parent of a six-year-old who asked you to explain your motives for entering this partnership, what would you say? What would a person for whom you have deep respect (your mother, your mentor, your best friend) say about this partnership?
- Partnerships need a business objective as well as a human or interpersonal component. Even a smart business alliance can fail if the human relationships are flawed. Conversely, partnerships between people who work well together can end prematurely without a business reason to sustain them. Is your motive for this partnership more business or personal? What does your choice suggest to you? What are the potential liabilities of your primary motive?
- What might the partnership need that one of you may have too little of?
- What might the partnership need that neither of you has, that you need to find, fund, borrow, barter, or create?
- What might the partnership need that you have too much of, the oversupply of which may create a problem?
- What might the partnership need that one or both of you possess but are reluctant to reveal for fear of being used, abused, undervalued, or exploited?

Now that you have taken an overview look, you are ready to consider six deeper questions anchored in the core protocols we discovered in our research.

Expect the Best
Is this a partnership that has the potential for bringing out the very best from all involved?

Be All, There
Do all parties have the capacity to be *totally engaged* when the partnership requires committed energy?

Assert the Truth
Can this partnership withstand the scrutiny of a bone-honest standard of behavior?

Honor Your Partner
Does this partnership appear to have the potential for bringing respect and honor to the parties involved?

Keep Your Promises
Will this partnership be laced with reliability and fidelity?

Stay . . . on Purpose
Can those involved in the partnership have sufficient commitment to the mission of the partnership that they demonstrate tenacity and persistence?

After thoughtfully considering all our questions about partnership, summarize your self-assessment by completing the following sentences:

- This partnership will give me (us) such advantages as . . .
- This partnership will probably limit my (our) opportunities by . . .
- The idea of partnering leaves me (us) most concerned that . . .

- This partnership could be the right approach for me (us) because . . .
- This partnership could be the wrong approach for me (us) because . . .
- What I like/dislike about my partner is . . .
- What I really, really want from this partnership is . . .

Focusing Past the Dream

Great partnerships start with the right focus and fit, but there's often more to look for than that. "Try to find out the sponsoring ideas underneath the dream for the partnership," advises Marjorie Blanchard, chairman of the board of Blanchard Training and Development.

> Very often there are reasons below the hopes and dreams. It's kind of like the tip of the iceberg which even the parties may not be totally aware of, about what could happen if this partnership were successful. It is only if you can get to that level of discussion, a more foundational level, that you really have alignment. It helps ensure you are partnering for the right reason.
>
> One time we were looking at bringing a company into a closer alliance and were talking about ways that we could co-market. I asked this person, "What if this thing were wildly successful, what would be happening to you personally that is not happening right now?" This person had an idea in mind that she would be able to earn the same fees Ken [Blanchard] was earning at that point, meaning her daily fees would more than triple. This was a point that had never come out in early conversation.

I said to her: "If you are aligned with our company and we are marketing you, we are going to have to take a part of that fee, which means you will have to book X amount to earn what you are describing." It suddenly became clear to her that her real reason for a partnership would never realistically materialize. Without exploring the sponsoring idea beneath the dream, our partnership would have been a major disappointment and failure.

Great partnering is not a contract, treaty, or deal—although these can be a part of the relationship. The purpose of partnering is to create neither a mutual admiration society nor a "you scratch my back and I'll scratch yours" arrangement. Defining partnering in such superficial terms would be like characterizing a dance as simply "moving to music" or "a performance art form." A partnership is a purposeful relationship that expresses a particular attitude and perspective.

LESSON

Understanding What Makes a Great Partnership

2

THINK FOR A MOMENT ABOUT SOME OF THE CLASSIC SONG-and-dance movies you've seen—*Singin' in the Rain*, *West Side Story*, *Grease*. A key figure in the creation of these motion pictures is the storyboard artist. This person, with drawing pencil and sketch pad, illustrates the screenplay—that is, draws what the camera sees in each take. The result looks like a giant comic book with the script under each frame. This artwork gives the actors, director, and film crew a common picture of how the movie will look.

We wondered what a storyboard artist would draw if the screenplay were the saga of a great partnership. What are the characteristics of great partnerships? Use the word pictures in this chapter as a checklist for the components that make partnerships last and last.

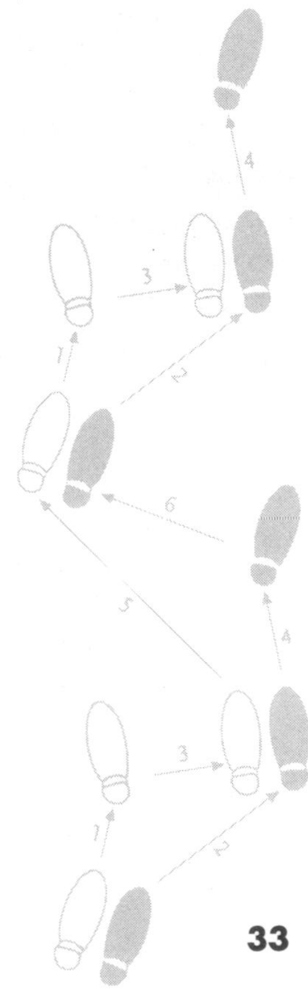

Great Partnerships Are Generous

Great partnerships are characterized by generosity—an abundance mentality and a giving attitude that willingly, even eagerly, go beyond the basic requirements.

Great partners don't keep score. And they don't compete for the benefits of the partnership, because they believe there's no limit on the benefit to be derived: the more you give, the more there is.

Frank Esposito, president of Tucker Rocky Distributing, puts it this way:

> One partner or the other will always have an opportunity to gain something at the expense of the other partner. It is a wonderful sign when the one who stands to gain comes to the other partner, acknowledges what is out there, and says, "We're in this together. . . . I am not going to do this as a single-minded opportunist."

> ***"When you think about ways to give rather than get, you know that partnership is working."***
>
> —Jay Cone, Interaction Associates

A great partnership is founded on the idea that growth and prosperity come from the combination of the partners' talent and efforts. No one is concerned with how the day-to-day benefits are distributed, because things even out over the long haul. Ted Townsend, president of Townsend Engineering Company, gave us a great example:

> Several years ago we were approached by a small family business who had come up with a new way to create sausages. We came to know and admire the founder father and his three sons. The father was diagnosed with cancer. Over time, we arranged to buy his invention and hire his sons. Now, after his death, the ongoing partnership with the younger generation has been wonderful. The sons are in marketing and introduce their father's

product with our updates to the world. It isn't just business. It is up close and personal.

Great Partnerships Are Trusting

To function well, a partnership must be grounded in trust. Partners cannot work while looking over their shoulders; they must be able to rely on each other to do the right thing. Says Perry Miles, president of Spirit Cruises: "There's an old saying, 'I'd go back to back with him in a bar fight.' Partnerships work when partners know their backs are being protected."

Trust implies reliability, assurance, faith. It means a partner is as good as his word. Partners waste no time or energy worrying about neglected responsibilities or broken promises. Instead, they invest their time and energy into managing high-risk, high-potential situations because they can count on each other to protect their common interest.

Ed Novak, CEO and founder of Broker Restaurants, gives an example of how partners demonstrate trust:

> When I began my first Broker Restaurant, one particular person behaved as a partner in the business from the beginning. He was not a manager or chef. Jerry Fritzler was a busboy. Over the years, Jerry learned to do every job in the restaurant. As time and the business progressed, so did Jerry. He learned wines, became a wine steward, an assistant manager, then a manager.
>
> At some point, I opened a second restaurant. In that restaurant, I had another employee who earned my trust, a food server named Kris Thompson. She, too, worked her way up to being a restaurant manager. Knowing the value of Jerry and Kris, I did not want lose them. So, for

"Trust ought to be so much a part of the essence of the partnership you don't have to even talk about it. It's like air. We take it for granted if it's clean and pure. Trust is like that. If you have to have a conversation about trust, it probably means something has gone wrong."

—Jay Cone, Interaction Associates

> one dollar, I sold each of them 25 percent of the ownership of the restaurant in which they worked. To be honest, my fear was that they would make all sorts of changes—which, as owner-managers, they had the right to do. However, my instincts were validated when they made very few changes. I realized what a great partnership we had developed over the years.

"Partnerships require a big-time investment. You must be proactive and not take the relationship for granted. Since so many things can undermine their effectiveness, limit your number of partnerships so you can invest the time and have the patience to grow the ones you have."

—Terry McElroy, McLane Company

Jerry and Kris echo the same sentiment. "I had lots of growing pains," says Jerry, "and Ed could have just sent me back. Instead, he trusted me and made a success of me. When our opinions differed, we had a common set of values to stand behind: Is it good for the guest? Is this the best we can be?"

"We looked past the immediate to the long term," explains Kris. "We did not make decisions on emotion or get caught up in the good or bad of the moment. Inside, this restaurant was 'my baby' long before I was an owner-manager. This is personal!"

Great Partnerships Share a Dream

Partnerships need to be bolstered by mutual vision. Though they rarely write them down, great partners nurture dreams of how great their association could be, dreams that more often than not coincide with or substantially overlap their partner's dreams. Shared visions foster harmony and balance.

The shared vision of a great partnership is not a simple agreement on mundane operations and objectives; it is a grand vision of philosophy and promise. The expected gains need not coincide, for each partner may find different immediate rewards in the relationship, and each partner may contribute benefits that the other partner is uniquely seeking. But partners must share the collaborative vision that is the hearth on which all the rewards are forged.

"It takes a total commitment to a common goal," Terry Pearce, author of *Leading Out Loud*, told us. "Not only are the values the same in great partnerships, but partners make it clear what it is they hope to do together. Some people call it a vision, some call it something else. Whatever the label, they should be very clear on their hopes and dreams."

> ***"Partnerships work long pull when their collective aim is noble, when their connection is compatible, and when the relationship is God-honest throughout."***
>
> **—Bob Ellis, *Daily American***

Great Partnerships Are Honest

Effective partnerships are coalitions cemented by truth. Honesty and candor are used not as weapons but as tools for growth. Great partners value authenticity and openness; they serve each other straight talk mixed with compassion and care.

The path to truth in relationships is through interpersonal risk taking and mutual critique. It involves the courage to ask for feedback as well as the compassion to give feedback effectively. Truth may sometimes leave relationships temporarily sore and edgy, but eventually it makes partnerships hearty and healthy. It is the quality that exterminates guilt and deceit. Truth nurtures cleanness in associations.

"Do what you say," advises Syd Kershaw, VP of Parker Hannifin, headquartered in Cleveland. "Live up to your partner's expectations." But honesty and truth are not just about being reliable and doing what you say. "Honesty is also being *able* to do what you say," says Kershaw. Boyd Pollard, CFO of Power & Telephone Supply in Memphis, sums up honesty this way: "The worst mistake you can make is trying to fool your partner. If you play games with your partner, you will be found out. It is never worth it, even if you can personally live with the deception."

Seven Ways to Stub Your Toe

Toe Stubber #1: Following the Crowd
Partnership is "in" these days. As a result, some partnerships are created more for show than for function. You can be justly skeptical when you hear someone talk about "having a partnership" rather than what the partnership achieves or how it benefits the partners. It's probably more for the annual report than for the southeast corner of the balance sheet.

Toe Stubber #2: Trust Me!
Beware the hard sell from a potential partner—especially from one whose resources and talents obviously don't balance yours. You may become someone's trophy partner, a tool for another's greed. Watch out for glowing generalizations about the advantages of coalition coupled with evasiveness about your actual benefits. A good partnership will give you good feelings, but they should be based on a realistic assessment of the success that can be achieved.

Toe Stubber #3: "Till Death Do Us Part"
Partnerships are, by nature, temporary arrangements. Many last a long time, but most reach a natural end once the mutual benefits begin to wane. Unrealistic expectations about the longevity of a partnership can cause partners to miss the cues for a graceful exit. When the relationship finally does end, often it is in bitterness and cynicism.

Toe Stubber #4: The One-Night Stand
A single-purpose transaction is not a partnership. Despite the current rhetoric, a customer is not a partner, nor is a single-transaction vendor. The customer's needs should be satisfied immediately, not over the long term. Most customers do not want or expect intense devotion in every service encounter. You might consider your accountant your partner, but you don't want an intense, long-term relationship with the kid at the car wash.

Toe Stubber #5: Organ Donor Needed
Some potential partners, even in an existing partnership, want you to come aboard to help them overcome a severe deficiency. They assume that allying with a healthy partner will solve their problems—or at least provide them with someone to share their misery. Unfortunately, the result is usually an unwell partnership with one more partner.

Toe Stubber #6: The Conventional Wisdom
Partnerships that lose sight of their ultimate purpose are often hobbled by convention, by what the partners perceive as the disapproval of others. Sometimes the purpose itself meets disapproval. But great partners must be bold and keep the courage of their convictions. They must dance their own dance and have faith that it will come out all right in the end.

Toe Stubber #7: Blind Loyalty
"We've always used them . . ." is often the first clue. "They know us too well . . ." is another. These expressions usually signify a relationship that doesn't necessarily work but is too entrenched to break. The ad agency, banker, accounting firm, or consultant who always seems to have a place at the table can be a sign of stagnation.

Great Partnerships Have Balance

To work together effectively, partners must feel that their efforts and rewards are distributed fairly. This does not necessarily mean that every aspect of the partnership is divided evenly or that there is moment-to-moment equality—just that everyone sees the overall relationship as balanced and equitable over time.

Chip describes his partnership of several years with a brilliant consultant who was ten years his senior:

> Our partnership began as a student-teacher relationship, far from equality. His late night debriefing sessions were laced with lots of "you should have's" and "why did you's?" But then I grew up! Our relationship struggled toward a more equal balance. However, my partner seemed unable to adjust to a partnership of equality, of true give-and-take. If I tried to offer him feedback, it was met with silence, defensiveness, and rationalizations like "Someday you'll understand." And his critique of my work began to communicate as much bite as betterment.
>
> As some of the clients we shared began to view their relationship with me more positively than their relationship with him, he accused me of deliberately trying to undermine his client rapport. Eager to show off my developing skills with all my clients, I failed to understand just how powerfully I threatened his place in relationships he had started and later generously shared with me.
>
> As our professional relationship began to deteriorate, our personal relationship became increasingly strained. Ultimately, we went separate ways, not as enemies, but as non-friends—a completely estranged relationship. I still miss his genius.

> ***"The partnership is in jeopardy when give-and-take becomes take."***
>
> **—Sherry McCool, St. Louis Marriott Pavilion**

"Solid partnerships are based on love, friendship, and caring," says Geoff Bellman, a Seattle-based consultant and author of *Your Signature Path*. "There must be mutual cooperation, trust, and equality." Says Brookfield Management Services' John Campbell, "If each gives more than 50 percent, you are well on your way to building a solid partnership foundation."

Great Partnerships Are Graceful

In a great partnership, the spirit of common purpose and action has an artistic flow that gives participants a sense of familiarity, comfort, and ease. Spend time with couples who enjoy great marriages, and you come away with a new appreciation for the meaning of serenity. The same is true for parents who are fortunate enough to have solid relationships with their children. While there may be occasional conflicts, the norm is dissonance-free calm and anxiety-free composure. There is a seamless ease and repose that we label "grace."

"One of the hardest parts of partnerships is not giving up when your toes get stepped on."

—Sherry McCool, St. Louis Marriott Pavilion

"Powerful partnerships are those in which there is no seam between where you end and they begin," says Chris Calabrese, general manager of the Marriott CasaMagna in Puerto Vallarta, Mexico. "When you think of your partner as a division of your own company, it's a powerful partnership."

Kevin Freiberg, coauthor of the best-selling book *Nuts! Southwest Airlines' Crazy Recipe for Business and Personal Success*, says, "Superior partnerships have an efficient eloquence about them. There is a seamlessness, or at least it looks that way, like world-class figure skaters, working their butts off to make it look effortless. Great partnerships are partners who know each other so well they can anticipate their every move and magically respond with accuracy and poise."

Are generosity, trust, shared vision, honesty, balance, and grace the only attributes of this dance we call a partnership? Of course not. Partnerships are growing entities undergoing continual change. However, if you assertively manage truth, trust, grace, and the rest as you reach for your collective dreams, then the parts we've failed to mention are likely to be unimportant.

Fancy Footwork for Focusing

Partnership greatness is not about finding the right partner; it is about forging the right partnership.

Partnerships survive because they have reason enough.

Like a doctor who begins a physical exam with a mental picture of a healthy body and searches for discrepancies, partnership assessment starts with a mental picture of great partnerships.

A partnership not worth assessing is not worth assessing well.

STEP TWO

"I have never worked a day in my life alone and never intend to. I work better with a co-choreographer, especially one who is strong in all the things I'm not, so that we make, together, one great choreographer."

—Michael Bennett

DANCE LESSONS

AUDITIONING

Picking Great Partners

He looked like the perfect partner . . . tall, muscular, graceful as a gazelle. She recalled the arduous acrobatic moves in the dance number that contained her shining moment in *Grease.* As Rizzo, the leader of the Pink Ladies, she needed a dance partner who would help her project a cocky charisma–the key to her future fame.

They slowly walked through the steps of the long jitterbug scene at the senior prom—there were lots of fast turns, showy throws, and flashy footwork. He seemed to catch on, but . . . she noticed that once or twice he zigged when she zagged. "Maybe he'll settle into his part when the tempo picks up," she silently hoped.

Do You Have the Capacity to Be a Great Partner?

Answer these questions candidly and thoughtfully. Your aim is to audition yourself to get a clear and honest understanding of the talent you bring to the dance.

What is your passion? Why are you really dancing this dance?

Recall a relationship that brought you joy and fulfillment. What assets did you bring to that relationship? What did people brag about?

If participants in the relationships of your life were to write your epitaph, and their goal was to capture the essence of the gifts and strengths you contribute to important relationships, what might they say?

When you are a part of a work team, how do you typically contribute, participate, or engage in it?

What are the positive adjectives your close friends would use to describe you?

Recall a moment when you gave more than you received. What impact did that contribution have on others?

What is it about relationships and partnerships that most sparks your excitement and passion? Your interests and curiosity?

What are the lessons you hope to learn from your next partnership? What lessons can you help teach?

If your potential partner were looking to you as an example or living model of some core value or principle, what might they see in you? How might they be pleasantly surprised?

What one personal virtue are you most enthusiastic about sharing with your potential partner?

Then the stage manager called for "places" for the prom number. It was *her* big scene!

They began okay. But their routine quickly deteriorated. His stride was way too short, his turns much too slow. He seemed to be dancing a fast waltz, not the frenzied shuffle the number required. He was winded after two minutes . . . and there were still four to go. He almost dropped her during a vigorous spin, just as the director salvaged some of her self-respect by screaming, "Stop!"

"Why did they choose him for his face, not his feet?" she moaned to herself. "I'll be in the chorus for the rest of my career!" They were worse than mismatched. It was a coalition that couldn't be corrected, no matter how many hours they put into rehearsal. "I should have known better . . ."

It is possible for two dancers to have clearly different strengths and styles and still perform effectively together, like the classic scenes in *White Knights* when legendary ballet dancer Mikhail Baryshnikov and tap dance great Gregory Hines teamed up. But if you are in your partnership to waltz your way to prosperity and your partner is set to do some serious line dancing, one of you is destined to get your feet stepped on. Auditioning is the step that helps you reduce your chances of limping away from a disastrous match.

YOUR FIRST AUDITION

Great partnerships have the same elements as great dance performances. "Great partnerships look easy," says Horst Schultze, president of Ritz-Carlton Hotel Company. "That's one way you know they are working. But behind what you see on the outside is a lot of hard work on the inside. So, you'd better start out with everyone having the same idea of what it's going take to make it work." Knowing what it's going to take to make it work starts with knowing your own attitudes and aspirations.

By "auditioning yourself" with the checklist here before you start sizing up your prospective partners, you can enrich your appreciation of the unique resources, skills, and talents you bring to the partnership and get early warnings of potential gaps, blind spots, and—as a Texas cowboy might say—"piles not to step in!"

And your auditions with prospective partners can get a shot of confidence by your starting in a good place. You have a better chance at partnership greatness if you begin with a keen awareness of the strengths you offer.

FINDING YOUR MATCH

Great partner selection is an absolute if your dance is to have symmetry, harmony, and grace. You never dance your best when you are preoccupied with whether your partner is likely to step on your feet or drop you in a challenging twist or turn.

In sizing up prospective duos, the dance world speaks of "fit"—meaning "they belong to each other." Partnership fit is obviously about matching up goals and values; fit is also subtly about matching style and rhythm.

Goal and value fit requires a precise match. There is no "sorta fit" or "almost fit" when commitment to goal and allegiance to values are involved. Mismatched goals and values, even if just slightly off, will beget bumps that ultimately become grinds.

Harmonizing style and rhythm is a very different matter from trying to reconcile conflicting goals and values. Matching style and rhythm is about creating symmetry, not sameness; you seek congruence, not to be carbon copies of one another You *can* dance with a different style dancer—but your path to harmony will be much harder.

> ***"One of the hardest parts of beginning a partnership is deciding who you are going to dance with and getting up the courage to ask."***
>
> **—Sherry McCool, St. Louis Marriott Pavilion**

Having vastly different styles also means that achieving symmetry will require accommodation and adjustment. When we started writing this book, our goals and the values we hoped to weave into it were identical. But our book creation styles are very different! While we gained from our dissimilarities a much richer appreciation of what makes great partnerships great, we had to work hard at bringing an elasticity to our partnership to meld our very different working styles.

MAY I HAVE THIS DANCE?

To help you make a good match, we have identified a few challenging "dancing" styles you might use in sizing up prospective partners. While each has its strengths and weaknesses, we have focused more on the drawbacks of partnering with each style and included a few suggestions on how to deal with them if you find you must join up with one of these more difficult characters. Remember, a goal in entering into a partnership is to stretch yourselves, but not to the point of self-destruction.

Strutters

Strutters are filled with their own self-importance. They do not partner easily, preferring more of a one-up, one-down relationship. Generally, their infatuation with their own worth is somewhat understandable . . . they indeed have worthy offerings, and that may be a good reason to partner with them. But Strutters lock their gifts away in the chest of fear and doubt: they fear their worth is less than they would have others discover. The latches that keep you from opening the chest are arrogance and posturing.

Strutters are the ultimate prima donnas. They are the most destructive partnering style of all. If you audition a Strutter, do yourself a favor and let them go strut their stuff elsewhere. Strutters are the partners who will lead you down the path to antacids and attorneys' fees.

If you must dance with a Strutter, proceed with caution. Do your homework up front, including preparing detailed agreements and plans for working together. That done, there are a few additional techniques to minimize their poison.

While the Strutter's arrogance can sometimes be amusing and harmless, it can also be a barrier to learning and changing, both crucial to great partnerships. If you are obliged to partner with a Strutter, your task will be to help your partner discover that her or his strut is simply unnecessary in your relationship.

Don't react to the Strutter's stuff; remember that the egotism you witness has nothing to do with you personally. If the Strutter starts to experience his or her prancing as a waste of energy in terms of your reaction and interest, you are on the path toward eliminating it.

Provide the Strutter lots of affirmation. Be quick to compliment and slow to critique. Look beyond their faults to discern their needs. Find some component of the Strutter's strengths to affirm (and even in an imposed relationship you will find strengths in your partner if you look hard enough, or you would not have gotten this far down the partnership path).

Be specific, authentic, and positive in your feedback. Strutters can spot false flattery a mile away. Never be reluc-

"Trust your intuitive gut. If it doesn't smell right and feel right, it probably isn't."

—Frank Esposito, Tucker Rocky Distributing

tant to show your confidence. But keep it smooth and grounded, not flashy and superficial.

Break Dancers

Break Dancers are difficult, energy-robbing partners. Assertive energy is terrific; very aggressive partners, however, can devour the collaborative spirit that fuels partner passion and commitment.

Break Dancers push and shove. Their preoccupation with "their way" steals creativity from the relationship. While some may speak the words of cooperation, their determined, domineering actions communicate a different agenda.

Sometimes Break Dancers' brilliance, genius, and general pain-in-the-buttness can kick a project to a higher level. When Break Dancers step out to show their extraordinary abilities and talents, their hearts are usually still in the success of the show—unlike Strutters, whose goal is always self-applause. When real break dancers twirl and jump over and under one another, there is an energy in their performance that will stop and excite every crowd. You could do worse than to embrace the Break Dancer's genius. Just remember that they need you and they know it!

Break Dancers like to be in control. They rarely listen. When they do, it is only to gain data to use to make a point or teach a lesson. They use their charisma as a weapon; they also use humor as a booby trap. Humility—so important to unity and learning—is replaced in the Break Dancer with dictatorial determination.

You cannot disarm the Break Dancer by fighting fire with fire. Trying to out-dominate a dominator just turns communication into contest. And the Break Dancer has incredible physical stamina.

Your best approach is to be respectful and grounded. Be firm in your position, but stay open to compromise or giving in on small issues, anything not critical to long-term effectiveness. Ask "What is your goal?" and "How will this help our partnership?" frequently.

Your objective is twofold: first, to help the Break Dancer shift from a focus on tactic to a focus on purpose, and, second, to assist your partner in sharing responsibility for the relationship, not just chalking up points on a false scoreboard. Look for ways to incorporate the Break Dancer's needs, desires, or issues into your approach. Model great partnership.

Bunny Hops

Bunny Hops have one or more of these characteristics: they are shallow, they are pollyannish, or they are short-timers. Partners need depth, someone who is substantial and in it for the long term, but Bunny Hops are affiliation junkies. They enter partnerships in search of affection, acceptance, and approval. And they see partnership as a stage set for instant glory and achievement, so they tend to keep the relationship at a perfunctory, superficial level, fearing that depth will lead to conflict and conflict will result in rejection.

An even graver threat to the partnership is their short-term orientation. Bunny Hops almost always have extremely unrealistic expectations of a relationship. They come into it believing that the music will always be melodious, the steps always in sync, the audience forever applauding. Yet they are not willing to do much work or contribute what they said they would. When the reality of partnership life proves less than they dreamed

What You Don't Want . . .

A vital part of a great audition is knowing what you don't want in a partner. We have not offered many absolutes in this book. This is an exception: never start a partnership with a partner who has slightly different goals or values with the hope of changing the partner after the relationship is underway. Partners *are* malleable. But hoping for something as critical to success as goals and values alignment is foolhardy.

Although many of us select our own partners, in corporations partners are sometimes selected for us . . . like which advertising agency we use, or which architect will build our building. If "they" chose with whom you partner, be sure you agree. You can and must influence the "they" to change partners if you are not compatible with the choice. It is your dance. And their show won't succeed if your dance number doesn't work.

(and it always will), they look for a quick exit, usually parting with a rationale that faults everyone and everything but themselves.

Most Bunny Hops are not worth the investment if a short-term exit is inevitable, but for some partnerships there may be value in having a short relationship to move yourself along to a true dance. Many Bunny Hops have sufficient gifts to mine the worth that lies below their sense of unworthiness. And, like Strutters, Bunny Hops need affirmation. Give it to them straight, as you would to the Strutter, but coupled with great warmth.

Be willing to nurture Bunny Hops, especially at the beginning of the partnership when their anxiety *and* their congeniality are highest. Random acts of kindness and tangible gestures of admiration can quell the "Am I okay?" insecurities they typically hold.

Wallflowers

Wallflowers bring an overdeveloped sense of caution and concern to their relationships. And, while some conservatism can be good for a partnership, pure risk aversion can be deadly. Partnerships that ardently stick to the tried and true are not likely to grow and progress. And being perpetual worriers, Wallflowers can tell you twelve reasons something won't work faster than you can think of one reason it will. They tend to champion the status quo to a fault, demanding pounds of proof for any potential act of faith.

Understanding what makes the Wallflower tick can take a lifetime. So, it may not even be worth the try! The Wallflower ranks are filled with good souls who felt the pain of unrequited love too early in life. Some Wallflowers are folks who loved and lost one too many times. Or they could be people whose love affair with logic taints all affairs of the heart with suspicion.

Wallflowers get cautious for tons of reasons. However, under their cautious and oh-so-stable exteriors, they are likely to be solid citizens who could be good partners if linked with someone who values their position without taking their position.

Learn from their caution. Remember the ancient adage: You are not eligible to change my view until you first demonstrate you understand my view. Wallflowers have gifts waiting and wanting to bloom. Give them the benefit of the doubt. Listen for the message behind their words. Speak to their substance; don't react to their form. If convincing is your goal, make your arguments logical, thoughtful, and reasonable . . . a language they will comprehend. Ask for their opinion often. And don't take their lack of affect as a sign of disapproval.

Wallflowers are safe and often shy; they are not likely to be impulsive or impetuous. So Wallflowers may be the best of our oddities with whom to partner. They will dance well in the chorus line, adding depth to your partnership, but don't expect them to be the star of the show.

Tap Dancers

Tap Dancers are all sound and no substance. They possess far more veneer than value. The tricky part with Tap Dancers is their knack for seducing you to not look too deep beneath their excellent exterior. Tap Dancers often learn their moves as super-salespeople, and sometimes a great sales partner is just what you need. But their gift for gab or their flair for influencing often gains them access to stages beyond their capacity to rightly claim.

If you find yourself more than a little impressed with a prospective partner's style, do due diligence. Check out the goods. Ask questions that require super-authentic answers: "Tell me about a time you took on a project and blew it." "If this relationship fails, how will you feel?"

Tap Dancers typically have ulterior motives—not necessarily dark or sinister motives, but ones that will not make it into the light until well into the partnership. This can add weight to your partnership that can cause it to stumble and fall on its face.

As with Strutters, spend your time up front focusing on the details of your impending partnership. Do your partnership audition completely and thoroughly, and watch for

"I used to say casting is 75 percent of the choreographer's job. Now I think casting is 90 percent. If you cast the dance right so much of it is already done. . . . I'm working toward the point where I can just show up at rehearsal, and it'll all fall into place!"

—Tommy Tune, in *Conversations with Choreographers*

early cues that you are dealing with a "too good to be true" relationship. In the words of an old Waylon Jennings country music song, "Be careful with things that are just what you want them to be."

Casting a great partnership means looking not only for goals and values that dovetail perfectly but also for the right blend of talents and temperament. During your partner auditions, keep in mind the wisdom of Spirit Cruises president Perry Miles:

> *There are some people who you will still have to do business with but you do not want to be partners with them. Make an investment up front but don't substitute hope for judgment. Don't see a prince when it's not really a prince. After you kiss the frog and it starts changing, make sure it is a prince it is turning into. Invest effort up front without going to trust too quickly.*

LESSON 3

What Makes a Great Partner?

ONE OF THE PEOPLE IN THE AUDIENCE WAS CHIP. HE MADE his way to the front of the room to congratulate Heather on her presentation on partnership fundamentals: "You have the makings of a powerful book in that speech—and you should call it *Dance Lessons*." "Yes, *we* do," she said, "and we *will!*" Complying with Heather's Partnership Fundamental #12—"Skip coffee or a drink and go for food!"—they went to dinner to explore writing a book together. Over the next few weeks, the process of forming and nurturing their book-writing partnership crystallized the wisdom and warnings they wanted to share with their readers. Twelve months later, the book you're holding was ready to go to press, and now the author-partners appreciate even more how important it is to a great partnership to choose a great partner.

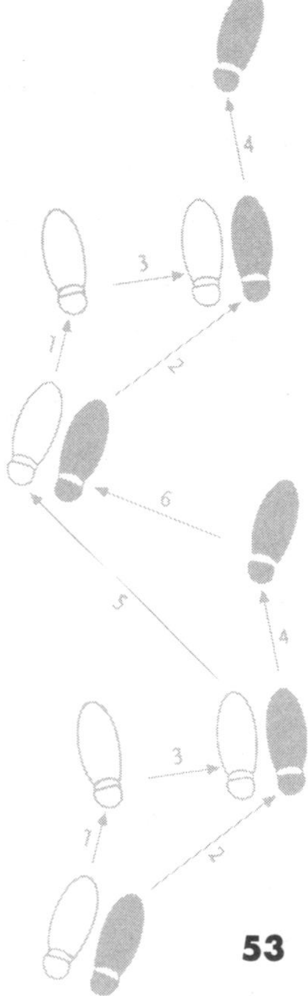

Heather on Chip
My company is named Inspiritrix. The word is derived from a Latin word that means "one who inspires another" or "dream carrier." Chip is a dream carrier. He pushes, pulls, and promotes me to live my dreams. He's also there when I need a friend, a good laugh, or even an ear to help sort out life's lessons. An extraordinarily talented teacher, he always treats me with the utmost respect, acknowledging my value both to him and to our partnership.

Chip on Heather
Heather is pure creativity. She looks at the world in a refreshing way, describing it with passion and enthusiasm. Her boundless energy and infectious brilliance fuel me to reach for greater heights. She has amazing instincts and can be bold in presenting them. When we met to work on the book, her ideas came out so fast we only captured some of them. We'll need to write a sequel!

"Partnership beginnings are all about finding someone you can be yourself with."

—Geoff Bellman, author of *Your Signature Path*

Great Partners Fill Gaps

"Show me the money!" was surely the most memorable line in the box-office hit film *Jerry McGuire*, but the second most memorable was the one Jerry uttered to his wife as he sought to reconcile with her: "You complete me." Or, as Stallone's title character in *Rocky* says about his girlfriend to her brother, who thinks she's homely: "I have gaps and she has gaps. We fill in each other's gaps."

Great partnerships exhibit this kind of completion. Each partner brings to the relationship capabilities and capacities the other partner lacks: resources, competencies, co-op buying opportunities, technologies, access. Thus, great partners seek partners who are their superiors in some ways. Rather than celebrating their own remarkable talents in glorious isolation, they choose to associate with others who surpass them in some of the capabilities and resources they must have to achieve their collective mission. They know that synergy is created by the partnership rather than the individual partners.

"Partnership success is all about compatibility," says Bob Ellis, managing editor of the *Daily American* in West Frankfort, Illinois. "If you're compatible, it's even possible to partner with someone you might not particularly like." Compatibility is characterized by John Campbell, president of real estate management giant Brookfield Management Services, in this way: "If [partnerships] work, it should be hard to tell where one partner stops and the other begins. And it's more than being 'joined at the hip.' It's about congruent values, common goals, and complimentary approaches."

"Passionate partners are more likely to succeed. They don't get complacent, they don't take you for granted, and they benefit all those around them."

—Javier Cano, Marriott Marina Beach

Great Partners Are Ready for Passion

Great partners are drawn to ecstasy. They are ready for passion, capable of being swept away—not gullibly, but in a purposeful openness to wonderment. They are primed to be enamored by the possible, treasuring the process as much as the outcome. And though they enjoy harmony, they take more pleasure in the energy of the encounter. As one senior manager said of his relationship with his counterpart in a supplier company, "Our partnership is sometimes easygoing and sometimes feisty, but it's always vigorous. I don't think I'd want a relationship that wasn't pretty much wide awake all the time."

"I'm on a mission in life to make a difference for women and people of color," says Eunice Azzani of New York–based executive search firm Korn/Ferry International. "I call myself a head farmer instead of a headhunter. I think if you really make a good match in the world, whether it is a person with a right job or a person with the right people in her life, that she is able to do greater things because of that partnership."

Great Partners Are Infatuation-Averse

Partnerships usually fail if populated with people who are simply "in love with love." There's nothing wrong with romanticism, but great partners balance their sizzling passion with a sound pragmatism. They know that after the initial fervor of the association cools, a partnership will rise to greatness only if there is a rational expectation of value-added benefits in its future. While the dance can swirl, it must also make sense.

Ed Novak, CEO of Denver-based Broker Restaurants, cautions, "Partnerships take time to grow. Solid partners slowly push the edge of the envelope. They allow time for the partnership to evolve and grow. This means you have to be very picky about who you select."

> ***"Not everyone is someone you will choose to partner with because partnerships take an incredible amount of time if they are going to work. So, be very selective. In fact, the hardest thing about partnership is remembering to go slow."***
>
> —Sherry McCool, St. Louis Marriott Pavilion

Great Partners Are Trustworthy

Great partnerships require partners with self-esteem—that is, partners who trust themselves. Partners who feel themselves trustworthy can find peace in the midst of turmoil; they will not tire of the intensity of the collaboration. They wear the robe of partnership like a tuxedo or evening gown, with confidence and pride. From this posture of strength, they are mighty enough to be weak, humble enough to be vulnerable, and confident enough to be authentic. Because they see themselves as worthy of trust, they trust others.

Trustworthiness means being comfortable with letting down one's guard and taking risks on others. Vulnerability becomes a strength in great partnerships because it opens the door to wisdom. "There must be an ease in the dialogue, a let-the-mask-down kind of innocence," says Charlotte, North Carolina–based Lynnwood Foundation president Sharon Decker.

Great partners not only tell the truth, they are its champions. They work as hard to learn the truth as they do to deliver it. "A breach of trust may not mean partnership disaster," says Jane Anderson, senior vice president of Saint Vincent Health System in Erie, Pennsylvania. "Betrayal is truly a painful experience for the partnership. But if you face the issue directly, honestly, and work through it, if you face the conflict with candor and compassion, you may end up with a relationship that is ultimately stronger."

"Unless you lay everything out on the table with me, I see a red flag. One of the biggest things is to enter relationships openly, honestly, truthfully."

—Tony Codianni, Toshiba America Information Systems

Great Partners Are Resilient

A good partnership takes resilience, tenacity, and patience. Great partners have good histories; they've lived through failure and learned from it, danced with pain and still love the dance. They derive success from two sources: a zeal to be the best and a desire to learn the most. Learning comes from failure, and success comes from learning. The continual cycle of failing, learning, and succeeding teaches great partners to be flexible, to be hardy, and to persevere.

Chris Calabrese, general manager of the Marriott in Puerto Vallarta, Mexico, tells of a failed relationship with a local rental car company that didn't persevere.

> The local representative did not connect with the global mission statement our two organizations had set up.

"If you keep anything secret from your partner, you are not truly being a partner."

—Bob Ellis,
Daily American

> When Mexico went through devaluation, we were having a hard time at this property, despite the fact that Marriott was doing great worldwide. They wanted to provide us half the number of vehicles we had agreed.
>
> We terminated our partnership. The city is now doing extremely well. Had that rental car company had the perseverance to hang in there with us, we would still be in a relationship, and a much expanded one.
>
> You have to stick together through the good times and bad. This is the test of a good partnership. When things get tough, you find out who the real partners are.

"Solid partnerships take a resilient attitude," says Saint Vincent Health System's Jane Anderson. "There will be struggles, rocks in your path. But through determination, a clear mission, and honest communication, the partnership should be able to get through most difficulties. Partnering is not for the fickle or the frail."

Great Partners Have a Deep Purpose

Great partnerships are made up of people who are set to go beyond "greater than" to a realm of "unforeseen worth." Great partners enjoy the quest for the best. Optimistic, intolerant of mediocrity, they expect the best table at the partnership banquet and assertively pursue it.

Great partners approach dissonance with a win-win orientation, not because it is popular, politically correct, or even productive. They've learned that a win-win approach is a faster route to depth—the reservoir for nobler purpose, deeper values, and durable worth.

Auditioning in Action

Cary: *"Oh, Dale! My assistant didn't tell me you were here! I would have insisted she ask you to come on in."*

Dale: *"That's okay! It gave me a chance to get caught up on a few phone calls. Nice office! You and I have the same computer. Did you get the 300 megahertz?"*

Cary: *"You bet! I learned long ago, always buy top of the line, since it gets obsolete so fast. You have the 300?"*

Dale: *"Yes, but mine only came with 32K of RAM . . ."*

Cary: *"This is your lucky day! I've got an extra memory expansion I can't use. Purchasing double ordered and I wound up with one I don't need. You take it!"*

Dale: *"Are you sure? It's just what I need. How'd they double order? Sounds like a problem if we do joint buying."*

Cary: *"I'm way ahead of you! We've already found the glitch and fixed it. Can I get you some coffee or tea?"*

Dale: *"Thanks, but I've had my caffeine quota. I'm excited about what this partnership might turn out to be."*

Cary: *"Me, too! But I'm anxious too. We tried an alliance once and got taken to the cleaners!"*

Dale: *"You sound like you're still pretty upset about it."*

Cary: *"You bet I am! It took us over a year to unravel the . . . but listen to me! We tried it, we blew it, we learned some lessons. But that has nothing to do with what we're starting here. Let's just forget I said anything."*

Dale: *"That's okay. What you learned can be helpful to us now. So I don't mind if you want to talk about it. But I'd feel better if you put down that letter opener!"*

"Getting your prospective partner to trust you is the most difficult part. You have to act the way any suitor would by doing the little things that show sincere interest before going for the big things—just as one might wait to meet someone's parents until one was sure the relationship was on the right track."

—Carlo Medici, Covance

Great Partners Assert Their Honor

Finally, great partners act in accordance with their most valued principles. They don't just go through the motions of establishing ethical standards, they live their code of honor, openly and assertively. The goal of great partners is not perfection; it is principled wholeness. They work hard to conduct themselves in harmony with their code, to make every move match their mouth.

> ***"Partnerships need people with high integrity. If the contract gets out of balance, it can be renegotiated. But partners without integrity, the 'talk the talk' type, are destined for failure."***
>
> —Jack Tester, Contractors 2000

Assertive honor requires a willingness to overcommunicate, to give partners more than the minimum necessary information. When partnerships fail, it is most often because of poor communication. Great partners communicate with clarity, accuracy, integrity, and regularity. This doesn't mean being a motor mouth; quality and frequency of communication is more important than quantity.

Great partners don't have to be super-heroes without flaws, doubts, or mistakes. A partnership is always a work in progress—it's perpetually taking dance lessons. The core of the dance called partnering is about growing, a mutual search for a synergistic kinship. As a collective pursuit, partnering works best when partners are more focused on building than boasting. The synchrony and synergy of partnering are what give it its dancelike quality.

LESSON 4

Conducting a Partnership Test: The Virtual Audition

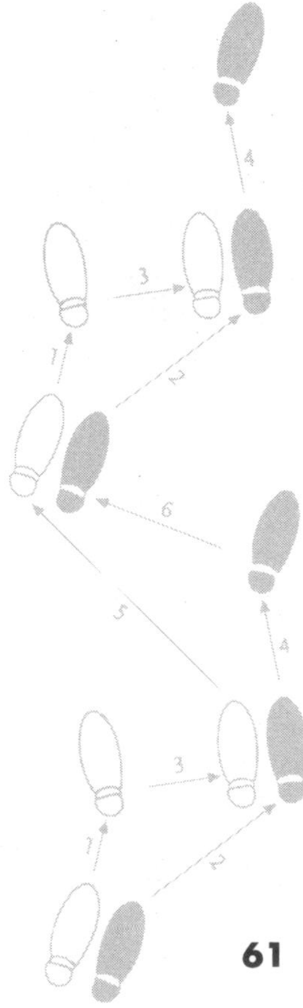

HOW MANY TIMES HAVE YOU HEARD DIVORCED FRIENDS lament, "We should never have gotten married in the first place" or "If I'd listened to my head as much as I listened to my heart, I would never have gotten into this relationship"? We are not necessarily advocating that those who intend to commit to relationships first live together. However, there clearly is a trial-run aspect to such an arrangement that could prevent later divorce.

Failed partnerships, like failed marriages, are often doomed from the start. How can business partnerships "live together" before they shake hands and say "I do"? Here's our solution: a partnership test.

This test will accomplish two things: (1) It will let you and your potential partner examine how compatible you are, and (2) it will reveal whether there is a rational purpose for your alliance. For these different objectives, the test has two parts: a virtual audition to test the soul of the relationship (lesson 4) and an eleven-point checklist to appraise the rational side of it (lesson 5).

Virtual Reality

Lesson 4 is designed to let you construct a simulated partnership. You and your prospective partner will candidly reveal early concerns, possible dead-end streets, and potential things to watch out for in the personality of the relationship. Most partnership due diligence procedures do not ask these questions up front; usually they anticipate only the rational, economic side of the relationship. This one-sided approach to assessing compatibility is, we believe, what dooms so many arrangements from the start.

We recommend that you start by examining the interpersonal side of the arrangement and its partners. Ask each other the questions; perform the outlined and suggested activities; reflect on your partner's answers and actions. Then, balancing idealism with pragmatism and passion with prudence, assess the results from your point of view.

Based on this tryout, how well will you and your prospective partner get along? How well will you work together toward your common goal? Passing this test is a good predictor of compatibility, an essential component of success. If you fail the test, our recommendation is that you skip the next chapter and look for another partner.

We have organized this virtual audition around the partnership qualities we outlined in Step One: Focusing. For each quality you will find

- **Key Questions** partners should ask each other in their due diligence interviews,

- **Activities** aimed at simulating partnership, and
- **Reflections** on your partner's answers and actions.

You will see a few questions in ***bold italics***. These are the "have to ask" questions derived from the core protocols we discovered in our interviews. Don't miss covering these vital issues.

The Value of Generosity, Quality, and Time

There are several important values that members of a great partnership must share. Three of the most important are their attitudes on generosity, quality, and time.

Generosity means that partners do not compete with each other. Instead, they find pleasure in extending the relationship beyond simply meeting a need or requirement.

Although quality, like beauty, is in the eye of the beholder, partners must agree on the definition and importance of quality in their personal and business dealings. Partners who want all A's will make strange bedfellows with partners who settle for gentlemen's C's. Out-of-sync values can lead to bitterness and resentment. Without alignment on quality, one partner will at some point feel cheated and want out of the relationship.

The partners must also share similar views concerning time. Punctuality, urgency, deadlines—all are flash points that can destroy a partnership. Most of us have had relationships in which tardiness, falling behind, or missed deadlines left us annoyed or angry. Countless partnerships fold because of dissonant views of time. As Parker Hannifin's Syd Kershaw says: "You know the partnership is working when schedules are kept."

"It is very important you have a strong set of core values. Values you practice every day. For us, it is honesty, integrity, loyalty, and high quality service."

—Dee Miller, USAA

> *"Look to fill in your weaknesses with their strengths."*
>
> —Bill Bolling, Atlanta Community Food Bank

Key Questions

- How often do you go beyond what your customers or associates expect in a relationship?
- How often do you do little extras for customers or associates just for the heck of it?
- If you had a forced choice between great quality late or adequate quality on time, which would you select?
- How often do you take a loss to help out a customer?
- What is your emotional reaction to missing a promised deadline?
- What is your emotional reaction to delivering lower quality than you promised?
- How do you usually react to associates whose attitude you consider selfish or greedy?
- Which of the three failings above (missed deadline, poor quality, or obvious greed) is the biggest hot button for you?
- ***How important is being the best to you? What would previous partners say your attitude about this is?***

Activities

- For no particular reason, buy a personal gift for your potential partner, present it, and note your partner's reaction (as well as your own).
- Find a favorite article on quality, give it to your potential partner, and schedule a time to discuss the article as well as its implications for your partnership.
- Eat dinner together (not just drinks or coffee). Go to the zoo together or take a long walk. Meet your partner's friends, co-workers, and other partners.

Reflections

- What steps will you take if you discover this partner has more greed than you have?
- What actions will you take if you feel used by this partner?
- How does this partner treat people at lower levels, with less money or less status?
- Recall what you remember about this potential partner's office, car, or home. Which items were most telling? Which gave you pause? Which gave you confirmation? Which left you puzzled and in need of more information?
- What did your partner not say that left you concerned?
- Are you willing to be unselfish?
- What actions did your potential partner take that left you feeling confirmed, concerned, or confused?
- What felt too good to be true? What surprised you and made you smile?

The Force of Truth

Partnerships that work share information copiously, beyond expectations. This includes sharing secrets, not so much out of obligation or reciprocity as from a desire for baggage-free interaction. Coming clean is not always comfortable, but it beats straining to keep secrets. And it fuels constant mutual learning, a prerequisite for great partnerships.

"Both parties must come to the table honestly," advises Jack Dowling, CIO of CompuCom. "It is vital they set expectations, talk about where the trouble might be, and start with caution. Even falling in love is with caution at first. You must be willing to share your strengths and own your limitations. If nobody confesses the truth, you are destined to fail. It is pay now or pay later, and later is always more costly than now."

"'Truth Rules' is the motto of our company," says Ted Townsend, president of Townsend Engineering Company. "You have to have the courage to speak the truth. When conflicts come up, you put the honest approach out there. You can tell very quickly if people are comfortable or not with that approach. If they are not, watch out. You will probably pay for it later."

"One of the things that I think is both the greatest strength and greatest weakness in a partnership is the differences people hold when they form a partnership. These differences can be very frustrating. They can also be a wonderful asset if partners know how to manage them. When they don't manage them and when two people always think the exact same thing, then one of them isn't contributing."

—Ellyn Bader
The Couples Institute

Key Questions

- Recall a time you were in a partnership when honesty became an issue. Reflect on your actions. What can you tell me that might teach me your approach or attitude?
- If your teenager picked a business day at random and could secretly watch you in all your business relationships, reading your intentions and beliefs as well as observing your interactions and behavior, what would she or he learn about your honesty and allegiance to clean, candid dealings?
- What areas of partnership do you find most difficult to be completely candid about?
- If "little white lies" or half-truths happen in our partnership, what are the areas in which they are most likely to occur? Why might they occur? What function would they perform?
- ***In your opinion, should partners be totally honest about* all *aspects and components of their partnership dealings?***

Activities

- Ask your potential partner for information about a previous partnership that may be helpful for you to know about that your potential partner has never shared with anyone.
- Ask your potential partner to tell you about a partnership strength that he or she brings but which you might not be likely to learn until you were in the partnership a while. Do the same with a partnership liability.
- Pretend you found a large sum of money that couldn't be traced to its source. What would you do with it? What would your partner do with it? Are your responses pretty much the same, or different? How do you feel about the similarities and differences in your responses?

Reflections

- Assume you will be stranded on a deserted island for ten years with this person. Will your partner be candid? How will you react?
- When you discuss the partnership, are you and your partner equally forthcoming, or is one of you more willing to be candid than the other?
- What did your partner not say that left you concerned?
- What actions did your potential partner take that left you feeling confirmed, concerned, or confused?
- Does your partner invigorate you or drain you?
- Based on what you know at present, what makes you feel this way?

The Power of Collective Dreams

Partnerships need to have all parties dancing to the same tune; synergy comes more from similar hopes and aspirations than from closely matched goals or missions. Great partners share a vision of some future state that can be brought into being through the alliance.

A part of collective dreams is compatible values. Tony D'Amelio, VP of Washington Speakers Bureau, says, "In the entertainment industry, totally different personalities contribute to the creation of a 'gem.' In business, that translates to shared values in the broadest sense, a collaboration of talent. It's like songwriters at work, one on lyrics and the other on melody."

Congruent values make a partnership last; differences make it rich. "I don't want a clone," asserts Tony Codianni, director of training for Toshiba. "I want a partner who can bring to the table something that I don't have within my own organization."

Key Questions

- What is your overall purpose for considering this partnership?
- What do you hope to be in this partnership? What role to you expect to play?
- ***What partnership purpose would most keep you from considering leaving the partnership if the going gets really tough?***
- Pretend it is five years after this partnership has come to an end. What are the qualities you would like me to remember as being associated with your actions?

- Assume our crystal ball tells us that after this partnership comes to an end and the dust settles, it will be an absolute break-even proposition economically. What will your commitment be like?

Activities

List five or six great partnerships you know of that you would like your partnership to emulate—the relationship between an athletic team coach and its owner, for example, or CEO's of two allied companies, or famous movie partnerships (Ginger Rogers and Fred Astaire, Butch Cassidy and the Sundance Kid, Abbott and Costello). Beside each example, list a word, phrase, or sentence justifying your choice. Compare your list with your partner's. Explore differences in your visions of what your partnership could become.

Reflections

- Are your visions sufficiently in sync to be compatible?
- Where are the outer edges of difference between your visions? What might be the potential consequences of this difference? Might they result in work at cross-purposes? Unresolvable conflicts? Communication challenges with people who must work with (or for) each of you?
- What did your partner not say that left you concerned?
- Is this partnership likely to be fun? Are you turned on and passionate about what this partner can be or do?
- What actions did your potential partner take that left you feeling confirmed, concerned, or confused?

"It's no fun to dance with someone who dances all over your feet. Picking partners with common rhythms, goals, and values is crucial. You can't have one partner doing the tango and the other dancing a waltz. You will wind up dragging each other all over the floor."

—Jack Dowling, CompuCom

The Force of Trust

Trust comes from experience; experience begins with risk. In a great partnership, each partner must be willing to take risks, because until the relationship is tested, trust cannot be firmly established. This means both partners must be trustworthy and must demonstrate trustworthiness at every opportunity. It also takes a certain boldness and bravery at first, until experience replaces fear with confidence.

Trust is generally associated with integrity and reliability. But there is a deeper issue when partnership is the context. Trust is the way partners deal with disappointment when experience falls short of expectations. Every partnership has hiccups; effective partnerships work to reduce them and go forward with the relationship as strong as before, or even stronger. Trust is more about who you stand for than where you stand.

"Partnership hangs on trust. Partners need to be willing to reveal. Trust drives joint business planning. It enables the partnership to focus on finding solutions to problems, not blame for problems. No trust, no partnership. And, if trust starts to waver, then the partnership will not be successful."

—Terry McElroy,
McLane Company

Key Questions

- If I were to interview the last five people with whom you've had a partnership and ask them about your reliability as a partner, what would they say?
- In the context of a partnership, what does trust mean to you? What are examples of betrayal of trust? Where is our potential partnership most vulnerable to betrayal of trust?
- You know yourself better than anyone. What is there about you that I should watch out for?
- ***A part of trust is reliability—keeping your promises. On a one-to-ten scale, with ten being "keeping promises is a super-important value" and one being "you shouldn't count on me," what grade would you give yourself?***

Activities

Take a trust walk together and describe your feelings. Take turns being blindfolded and led around through unfamiliar territory by your partner. Then talk about the emotions you felt. More important, explore the implications of your emotions to a partnership you might jointly pursue.

Reflections

- What answers did your partner give that most surprised you? What might this imply for the partnership?
- Can you trust this partner's motives?
- What did your partner not say that left you concerned?
- What actions did your potential partner take that left you feeling confirmed, concerned, or confused?

The Merit of Balance

Great partnerships are interdependent alliances based on communal needs and goals. Great partners focus on mutual respect rather than rights; they recognize and accept differences. Instead of power and control, the relationship is based on communication and accommodation of expectations—a balance between individual desires and the common good.

Balance also encompasses cultural like-mindedness. When mores and mindsets are not in sync, one partner may perceive the other as abnormal. There are always differences between partners that must be accommodated, but too great a difference may never be adequately bridged, even by partners determined to be flexible and resilient.

> ***"Close partnerships are those that are in sync with the needs and desires of both partners."***
>
> —Dennis Bolling, Producers Livestock Association

Key Questions

- We all have our unique styles, our peculiarities and eccentricities. For example, I sometimes drive people crazy when I (name one of your oddities). Tell me about some of yours that will be helpful for me to know in our relationship.
- Partnerships require a certain amount of give and take. What are the areas or issues around which you will have the most difficulty finding a mutual or reciprocal approach?
- What does a balanced relationship mean to you? What does such a relationship look like to you?
- What are the areas in previous partnerships where you had difficulty giving up control? What were the factors? Describe a situation that provoked resistance.
- What are some ways I can help you or support you with this kind of challenge? If I give you feedback, are there words or phrases you hear more clearly or easily than others?
- ***If I interviewed your previous partners and asked them to describe you regarding "respect for your partner," what might they say?***

Activities

Select a customer in whom you are both interested. Pretend you need to write a letter to this customer on some sensitive issue (pick one). Together, draft this letter. (Alternatively, choose a cause or issue in which you share interest and write a one-page letter to the chamber of commerce, mayor, or governor.) Explore your emotions during the writing process. Focus on issues of leadership, control, and credit.

Reflections

- What worries you most about how your potential partner reacted to the activities?
- What early warnings did this experience give you?
- What answers did your partner give that most surprised you?
- What might this imply for the partnership?
- What did your partner not say that left you concerned?
- Are you willing to collaborate and compromise in this partnership?
- What actions did your potential partner take that left you feeling confirmed, concerned, or confused?

Uncommon Questions for Unusual Partners

If you think you may be partnering with one of our more challenging partner types, consider adding one of these questions as your situation requires.

Strutter

What suggestions do you have for managing our partnership if you discover that I'm much (stronger, more powerful, more influential) than you anticipated?

Break Dancer

I'm sure you would agree that effective partners are keenly aware of their strengths and limitations. (Wait for a "yes" before you continue.) What do you see as your partnering limitations?

Bunny Hop

What will be the impact on our partnership if you discover that I'm much more forceful and confrontational than you expected?

Wallflower

What will be the impact on our partnership if you discover that this partnership's success requires high-risk decisions and gutsy actions?

Tap Dancer

Tell me about a time you were in a situation that really made you anxious.

Dancers in auditions often feel cheated out of favored parts or roles when the scout fails to give them a chance to truly strut their stuff. But dance partners—and business partners—should use the audition as a chance to see not only their partner's best, but also their worst and their typical performance. And rather than create unrealistic expectations, partners should be willing to reveal their own standards and shortcomings.

Partners should remember that the showy passages are not the whole of the dance. We must be comfortable performing the journeyman parts, willing and able to keep the show going when the spotlight is elsewhere.

LESSON 5

A Partnership Test: The Eleven-Point Checklist

A GOOD AUDITION IS VITAL IN FORMING A GREAT PARTNERSHIP. It is an opportunity to begin learning from and communicating expectations to your potential partner. Participants can openly and candidly explore values, attitudes, and approaches—essential information for ensuring a smoothly functioning partnership. Specifics are important throughout. "Ambiguity can mean disaster," says Lillian Prymak of Executive Forum in Englewood, Colorado. "Discuss scenarios very early. Take the time up front to explore all the 'what if's'." Better to invest the time and effort into firming the particulars up now than to later find yourselves looking for a graceful way out. Then, as Producers Livestock Association's Dennis Bolling sums it up: "You are ready to begin a relationship when their need becomes your goal and they feel the same about you."

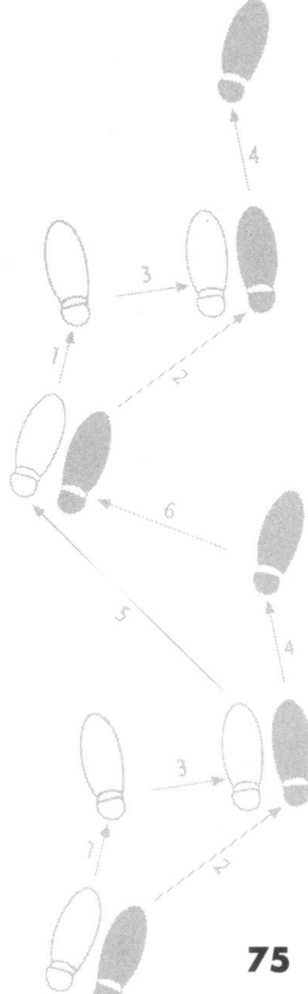

Point by Point

Assume now that you are confident you have the right partner. There is an important next step to be taken before you firm up your alliance. The questions in this eleven-point checklist are designed to help the two of you assess the rational side of your potential partnership.*

Although some of them may not be relevant to your present situation, they are important considerations for auditing your partnership's potential. Reviewing them together can reveal hazards that might later cause the partnership to stumble.

Checkpoint #1: Complementary Strategies

- Are our individual marketing approaches effectively served by this partnership?
- How can this partnership enhance or improve our strategies?
- If one of us is adversely affected strategically by this partnership, are there ways to compensate or support that partner?

Checkpoint #2: Cultural Congruence

- Are our cultures (what we believe, how we live, our norms, values, and styles) congruent, or at least compatible?
- Can our incompatibilities coexist without jeopardizing the partnership?
- Are there cultural changes down the road that could damage our partnership?

*Appreciation to Ron Zemke and Jim Kouzes for their input on these questions.

Checkpoint #3: Views of Time

- Do we have similar views of the future of our partnership? Have we been open about how long we expect it to last? Do we agree on how to end it satisfactorily?
- Are our philosophies on time the same? Does urgency have the same connotation and value for both of us? Are we equally fervent about meeting deadlines?
- Have we agreed on the consequences of delays or missed deadlines?

Checkpoint #4: Control Practices

- Do we measure, monitor, and inspect in similar or complementary ways? Do we have compatible ways to make decisions and solve problems?
- Are our record-keeping, accounting, and control systems and practices cut from the same cloth?
- Do we need to change the way we measure processes and results in order for the partnership to verify and gauge progress?

Checkpoint #5: Front-Line Information System

- Do we communicate alike unit to unit and person to person?
- If things go wrong, are our early warning and repair systems and skills compatible?
- Are our organizations structured to support this partnership? Have we talked about whether and how they can be improved?

"Partnership requires full and adequate disclosure. Partners must be willing to lay all their cards on the table—the good cards and the bad cards."

—Dennis Bolling, Producers Livestock Association

Checkpoint #6: Shared Values

- Is a win-win philosophy a normal part of the way we do business? Do we need to create a stronger, more obvious win-win philosophy in either of our organizations? Can we assertively talk about trust issues?
- Are our views on the meaning and importance of quality compatible? Will we approach quality assurance with similar tools and fervor?
- Are our customer service views and practices compatible? Will we approach understanding and meeting customer needs with similar tools and fervor? Does customer loyalty hold the same value for each of us?

Checkpoint #7: Goals, Roles, and Tolls

- Are we of one mind on the partnership's primary business goals? Are we clear on what we're trying to achieve together?
- Do we have the same view of the roles we (and our organizations) will play in this partnership? Have we talked about how we will handle conflict if our roles change after the partnership is under way?
- Do we have exactly the same view of the price of our partnership time, expense, resources needed, frequency of encounters and transactions, and other tolls?

Checkpoint #8: Compatible Intellectual Capital

- Within our units or organizations, do we each have the right skills and knowledge to manage this partnership effectively?

- Are there provisions for acquiring the intellectual capital that we need now but don't have? That we may need later?
- Have we talked about how we will deal with an unequal distribution of intellectual capital between us or between our organizations? Is the concept of continuous learning hard-wired into this partnership?

Checkpoint #9: Economic Reciprocity

- Do we agree on how to allocate the returns, profits, and benefits from this partnership?
- Have we talked about what we will do if the returns, profits, or benefits end up larger than we expected? Smaller? Different?
- Do we share similar views and practices on business ecology issues such as expense control, savings, productivity, waste management, and efficiency? Have we talked about how we will recognize and review incongruent practices?

Checkpoint #10: Respect for Privacy

- Do privacy and confidentiality mean the same to each of us? To each of our organizations?
- Have we talked about what steps we will take to recognize and review inappropriate encroachments on privacy or violations of confidentiality?
- Have we discussed ways to deal effectively with changing privacy needs after the partnership is underway?

- Have we talked about our respective opinions regarding the need to be totally honest about *all* aspects and components of our partnership dealings?

Checkpoint #11: Leadership and Control

- Will there be a leader in this partnership? Will leadership come from an individual or a team?
- Does this partnership need champions or sponsors? If so, what steps will we take to acquire and retain them?
- Have we talked about managing control within the partnership? How do we address inadequate control? Overcontrol? Inappropriate control?
- Do we know how we might handle differences in leadership? Have we talked about what we will do if one of us disagrees with the way the other is leading?

Intimate Inquiry

All the checkpoint questions are relevant for all types of partnerships. Partnerships requiring high levels of commitment, interdependence, and interpersonal bonds—like Tango partnerships, and sometimes Waltzers—may need to explore a few additional questions:

- How will we effectively manage the all-absorbing intensity our partnership may require?
- What will we do if others on whom we rely demonstrate jealousy regarding our close relationship?
- How will we signal each other if one of us desires to change the partnership to a form with less (or more)

investment (for example, I want to stop doing a Tango and start Square Dancing)?

- How can we ensure that our relationship does not get too serious, intense, or demanding?

Partnerships work when sufficient assets and resources are available to them. They have the potential for greatness when your attitudes and reasons for partnering are congruent. Great partnerships make a point of doing a sober assessment and straightforward agreement on what each brings to the dance.

Axioms for Awesome Auditions

Auditions start with warm-ups. The action should be directed toward creating a climate for openness, candor, and acceptance.

Everything happens in the beginning. Early encounters are a microcosm of the partnership's future. Pay attention.

Auditions are expressive. Listen intently to learn the feelings behind the words—then give responses that speak to those feelings.

Auditions are best served by authenticity and humility. The sooner you verbalize your feelings, the faster your potential partner will show matching vulnerability.

Falling in love is always irrational. "Falling in partnership" must reflect a proper balance of the logical and illogical. Auditions are meant to be a spirited discussion between your heart and your head.

STEP Three

DANCE LESSONS

"Dancing appears glamorous, easy, and delightful. But on the path to the paradise of achievement is fatigue so great the body cries, even in its sleep."

—Martha Graham

REHEARSING

Getting the Partnership in Shape

The theater was dark except for a small desk lamp on a table twenty feet out from the base of the stage. As the two young dancers entered from the lobby, they slammed on brakes to let their eyes adjust to the sudden darkness. The tiny light had an eerie look through the cigarette smoke curling from the man and woman seated at the table. Poring over a coffee table–size notebook, they were animated and noticeably edgy.

"It's too heavily weighted to the right," said the woman. "The chorus will take too long to reach

center stage if they have to go around that set. The audience won't be able to see them."

The young intruders quickly realized that the spirited people down front were the choreographers of the production in which they had a week earlier won a role. Today was the first day of rehearsal, and the eager dancers had arrived an hour early.

"Will you need one or two boom lights?" a voice yelled from stage left. "Two!" the choreographers answered in unison. They laughed at their sudden show of unanimity, and their mood lightened. "Let's take a break," the man said. "We can work some of this out when we start rehearsal." They closed the score, crushed out their cigarettes, and walked backstage.

Dances have a score negotiated and refined through fits and starts, trials and tribulations . . . just like partnerships. A real dance score is more than the dancer's version of "paint by numbers." There are notations that communicate the tone, pace, and spirit in which the musical accompaniment must be performed. There are drawings and symbols that telegraph stage layout, prop placement, and lighting arrangement and movement. There are both written and drawn instructions for the dancers that depict their positions on the stage and their alignment with the audience. Overlying the dance score are the customs, conventions, language, and norms universally understood by dancers, directors, and support people. This array of directions provides a clear picture of "the dance."

CREATIVITY THROUGH STRUCTURE

At first blush this "nothing left to chance" approach may seem to threaten to rob the performance of all creative expression. The opposite is what actually happens.

Creativity emerges from structure. Just as the skill of a great surgeon emanates from years of practicing the craft, just as the finesse of a champion poker, chess, or tennis player is squeezed from years of practiced protocols, dance is creativity sprung from structure. Out of a tightly choreographed foundation, dancers are released to deliver their creative interpretation that makes every performance both like the previous one yet completely different from all others.

Rehearsal is the step that you might want to rush through or skip. Don't. Like practicing your pliés or piano, thorough rehearsals are the key to great partnerships. As Peter Hall of the National Theater in London says, "Discipline will set you free."

BUILDING AN AWESOME ALLIANCE

We have studied countless partnerships famous for their long-term effectiveness and interviewed many of the participants in these admirable alliances. Our key questions have revolved around that unmistakable "state of impeccability" that is the mark of a great partnership: When your partnership was unquestionably hitting on all cylinders, what was happening? When your partnership was so smooth and flawless you seemed to be carried effortlessly by its energy, what was going on around you?

Describing an "awesome performance" is not easy. Great athletes struggle to describe that moment when mind-body-spirit and goal merge to create the "near-perfect performance."

The business partners we interviewed had a similar dilemma. They wrestled with words to wrap around their "beyond description" experiences in great partnerships. We heard phrases like "absolutely effortless," "flow," "magical," "mystical," "hot," and "not of this world" used to characterize the experience. Our dissection of the moment let us to conclude that five phenomena were happening simultaneously:

1. All partners possessed the *skills*, competence, or wisdom to carry out their part of the partnership.

2. All partners were challenged by a partnership *goal* that was crystal clear and viewed exactly the same by all concerned.
3. All partners relied on agreed-upon *cues* or pacts that they could trust to keep them on track.
4. All partners were effective at providing each other *feedback*, information that both advised the partners on the accuracy of their efforts and nurtured (that is, fed) the partnership.
5. All partners honored a set of *protocols*, those no-need-to-explain standards of partnership behavior that they could depend on, even in (most especially in) the most trying situations.

Assuming the partners had the requisite skills, it was the right conditions (goals, cues, feedback, and protocols) that positioned the partnership to express its soul, to enjoy that sparkly zenith of performance when everything clicks so well it awes even the participants.

REHEARSE, REHEARSE, REHEARSE

The lessons in our Rehearsal step are the longest. They are the disciplined work of powerful partnering. But this step is what makes the partnership dance effective and special. More tactical than inspirational, it contains the warm-up exercises you must do in order to not get hurt in performance.

Great dances do not occur spontaneously, in a vacuum. They work best when there is support and accompaniment . . . well-rehearsed music, an enthusiastic audience, and a well-suited partner. Likewise, partnerships work best when there is relevant skill or competence at partnering directed toward a challenging and pertinent goal, supported by advance agreements on cues, feedback, and protocols. We will label this combination of goal-cue-feedback-protocol "conditioning" and assert that without these aspects of conditioning, partnerships with the greatest intention and most spirited inspiration will likely falter or fail.

The Audition step explored the path to finding *skill*–how to determine both fit and fitness. In the next lessons, "The Conditions of Conditioning" and "Blocking Out Your Performance Together," we will interpret the four conditions that support great partnerships: goals, cues, feedback, and protocols.

Goals in partnerships are like goals in any other type of relationship. They point the union in a common direction, enabling your effort to be efficiently expended and finely focused.

Cues are the pacts, covenants, or special understandings worked out between the partners. These agreed-upon codes, winks, and nods give the partnership its unique character.

As an extension of the partnership's common vocabulary, cues allow you to customize your performance. Partnerships work well when you and your partner have discussed and agreed on your promises and deals. Suffice it to say, many partnership failings can be traced to poorly communicated agreements or to one or more partners' failing to keep the agreements they made.

The Components of Partnership Greatness

Talent	+	**Conditioning**	=	**Soul–The Basis of Greatness**
Skills		Challenging goals		Generosity/love
Capacity		Cues/covenants/pacts		Faith/belief
		Feedback		Trust
		Core protocols		

Cues, however, need ongoing work to keep them relevant. That dynamism happens through *feedback*. In other words, having a cue is only the first step. Partners must *use* the cue to keep it viable. And use requires feedback. Skill at giving feedback is therefore just as critical as competence in crafting agreements. And it is feedback that nurtures the relationship. When Ken Blanchard characterized feedback as the "breakfast of champions," the "breakfast" part was as vital to his description as the champion part.

Dances also have a language . . . a set of norms

or rituals that make dancing different from bowling. Norms and rituals give dancing its discipline. Likewise, partnerships have specific core *protocols* or conventions that give partnering its form and structure.

We believe that lack of partnership protocols—or partners operating in a relationship where they employ different protocols—is the culprit responsible for most partnership failings. Our partnership research uncovered key conventions or customs present in every great partnership, and they too will be explored as part of your partnership rehearsal.

Skill, form, and structure are only part of what makes a great dance performance. Above all, dancers have feelings that they express through the dance. Without the emotion of their expression, their dance would have no more vitality than the choreographer's diagrams.

Partnerships require soul . . . the energy or vitality of the relationship. They must be laced in love and generosity to contain the capacity for forgiveness and the commitment for loyalty they require. They need a sense of wonderment and faith to be open to surprise, innovation, and serendipity. They must have passion and inspiration to weather trying moments. They must perpetually focus on inclusion as the foundation for consideration and respect.

When these more spirit-full dimensions are added to the partners' conditioning and rehearsal, the stage is set for magic . . . that surprisingly rich flow of partnering in perfect motion.

LESSON 6

The Conditions of Conditioning

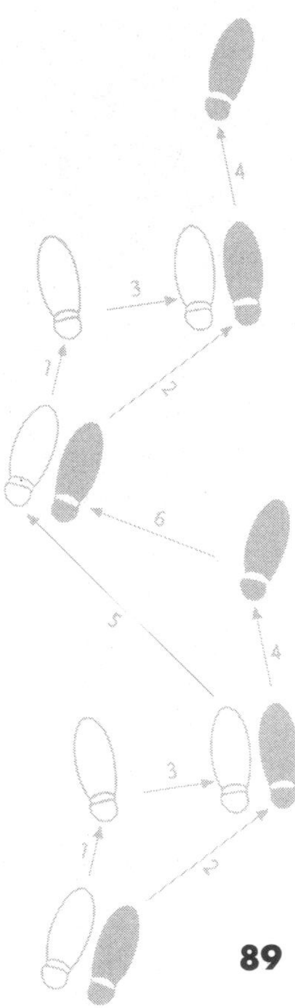

PARTNERSHIPS, LIKE DANCES, NEED TO BE REHEARSED IN order to succeed. In dance, rehearsals begin by communicating purpose and going through walk-throughs (as dancer and choreographer Gene Columbus says, "Dancers must know where they are going and why they are going there"). Then they focus on conditioning the dancers to work with and respond to one another as they refine their moves.

Conditioning is equally important in a partnership. It ensures the fluidity that gives a great partnership its efficiency and sharpness. It doesn't happen by accident. When people speak of a partnership having synergy, they are describing one of the results of conscientious conditioning.

Goals: Always Know What the Dance Is About

How does a real dance rehearsal begin? Wise directors open rehearsal by conveying the aspiration or aim of the dance. "Ladies and gentlemen, we are here for a single intent: to convey the magic of the night before Christmas to our audience," begins a ballet director. "The *Nutcracker* you will be performing is a timeless expression of a child's dream of Christmas Eve. Our audiences will be moved if we can convey the innocence and wonderment of that expression. They will be inspired if we can rekindle a feeling of nostalgia about their personal remembrance of things past."

Notice our hypothetical dance director's emphasis on tone and feel, destination and intent. Great partnership rehearsals are similar: they include an explicit expression of the goal of the relationship. Defining the goal of the partnership is different from understanding its purpose. Purpose tells "why"; goal explains "what." Partnership purpose proclaims a rationale and direction; goal communicates a destination and target. As the director states aim, style, and tone, partners must begin their rehearsal with a clear statement of objective.

Defining the goal helps partners create a common "big picture" in their minds. Although rehearsal begins by focusing on mechanics, in time the steps grow less important as they become more instinctive and unconscious. At that point the major moves, the big-picture goal, come to the forefront. The feel of the music becomes a more important guide than the technique of the step. Details remain important cues, but the ultimate focus is on flow and feel.

Making this transition, from the narrow view of technique to the broader perspective, can be trying. Partnerships stuck on the steps never enjoy the sweep of the grander flow.

Getting the Big Picture

It's important to begin by clarifying the ultimate goal, right at the opening of the rehearsal. The partners must create this big picture together; it serves as a touchstone against which all subsequent efforts and progress are measured, and it should be constantly reexamined.

How do great partners talk about the big picture? How do they decide what the 50,000-foot view of their alliance should be? We suggest a four-part goal-setting formula for guiding what can be an awkward opening: feeling, hope, goal, and promise. Answer for each other the following questions:

- What am I *feeling* right now? What emotion am I experiencing?
- What are my *hopes* for this relationship? If everything works perfectly, what are my desires?
- What do I see as the *goal* of this alliance? What are we trying to achieve with this partnership?
- What do I expect to bring to the relationship? What kind of pledge or *promise* can you expect from me?

> ***"Winning partnerships have a purpose, and the partners know it. You have to know your partner's main business challenges, how your partner's success is measured, and what your partner's hopes and dreams are. Meshed with your own, these form the basis of a purposeful partnership, not just a transaction."***
>
> **—Melinda Goddard, Roche Laboratories**

Rehearsing in Action: Goals

You will recall that Cary and Dale had gotten together initially in an exploratory meeting at Cary's office. They agreed to go forward with their partnership. The meeting we are about to hear was to agree on their working relationship—their "rules of engagement."

Listen to the sounds of the four-part goal-setting formula woven through their dialogue on partnership.

Dale: *"Cary, I'm glad we got some time to talk about where this thing might be going. You know me, I'm a straight shooter."*

Cary: *"Me too! We've got a lot on the line, my friend! If we don't get this thing off on the right foot, it could cost us."*

Dale: *"We can also make something terrific, given the opportunity."*

Cary: *"You betcha! I'm excited and I'm also a little anxious. Kinda like how you felt on your first date!"*

Dale: *"Now, don't be getting any ideas!"*

Cary: *"Aw, you know what I mean. I don't know about your folks, but my people are watching this thing pretty close."*

Dale: *"Mine, too! And I have those same feelings. But I have great expectations! I'm hoping we can create something together that can be a model for other ventures. If this one works, we might want to do others."*

Cary: *"I'm glad you said that. This does have a kind of pioneering side to it. What can we do to make that model you're talking about?"*

Dale: *"Well, I made a couple of notes here. Since our primary goal is to craft an approach to do joint purchasing and marketing, my folks can put together a couple or three 'best case scenarios' that you and I can review. If you can do the same, maybe we can settle on a structure we like."*

Cary: *"You got it! I'll also bring in some of the questions my staff asked out of the due diligence study. Since there's a public relations piece in the joint marketing goal, we need to be sure we're both singing from the same song sheet. You probably got a few funny looks from your study, like I did!"*

Dale: *"I'm glad you mentioned that. I didn't realize PR was a part of the marketing. We don't do much in that area, so maybe you all can teach us a few things. We do have a very large mailing list sorted forty-'leven different ways. I can send that over to you and you can decide what part you think should be done jointly."*

Cary: *"Sounds great! I'm already liking the openness we have. I'm a pretty close-to-the-vest person, but you have my word that I'll be as open and up front as I can be."*

"Start with very clear goals and extremely clear measures of accountability," advises Terry McElroy of McLane Company. "And remember that traditional measures don't work. You are looking at the long haul. We find if you do not see the kind of results you planned in about six months, reassess."

Our suggested formula should be considered a guide, not a script. We've found that this feeling-hope-goal-promise model combines several important affective factors, all tantamount to effective beginnings. Good beginnings have authenticity, a feeling that there has been a wholesome, judgment-free encounter. Good beginnings have optimism, an anticipation that all will go well. Good beginnings have purpose, a steadfast pursuit of some worthy accomplishment. Finally, good beginnings have an unwritten covenant to accomplish.

> ***"Most great partnerships do not happen by accident. It takes forethought and clear communication about values, vision, and expectations. It requires taking the time to generate future 'what if' scenarios. Solid partnerships handle the inevitable bumps well because they anticipated them, talked about them, and planned for their occurrence."***
>
> **—Kevin Freiberg, San Diego Consulting Group**

Cues: Communicating Agreements and Pacts

Great partners anticipate difficult times and set up plans to deal with them. They treasure early warnings, of course, but they *do* expect surprises. To deal with these surprises, they agree in advance on cues—signals or agreements that ensure that their interpersonal connections continue harmoniously.

Rehearsing in Action: Cues

Here is the scene of our two partners crafting what will become their cues. Their talk explores needs, expectations, and requirements—as well as each partner's habits and frailties—all aimed at preparing each partner to "pick up the slack" or "catch me when I trip." Cues start out spoken, but they should be recorded so that they can be reviewed and remembered.

Dale: *"Thanks for the heads-up on the Bianca deal. I think we'll get that business, thanks to your quick call."*

Cary: *"That's what partners are for! Besides, you've thrown a lot of new business our way. It was a chance for us to return the favor. Speaking of a quick call, your surprise tells me it was unusual for you to get a call that fast. It's sorta the norm for us."*

Dale: *"Well, we'd call fast in an emergency. But our standard is call-backs within twenty-four hours. Yours must be same business day."*

Cary: *"Actually, it's faster than that—four hours or less. We've found it gives us an advantage with some of our customers."*

Dale: *"We can work with that. Can you operate with a minimum amount of paperwork? Our organization favors face-to-face over calls, and calls over memos. My sense is that you're more paper driven.*

Cary: *"I'm pretty sure we can cut down on the paper, but it'll take some adjustment. And we may ask you for more documentation than you're used to giving."*

Dale: *"I'll brief my folks. Now, I have a thorny one. Your group has a reputation for being squeaky clean—and that's admirable. But our niche of the market can be a bit squirrelly, more gamy in their dealings. Not that we do anything illegal—but we do take poetic license*

> ***"Investigate thoroughly and develop a solid business plan that is not just based on the monetary side, but a business plan that is based on job responsibilities, and have it all inclusive, to include the partnership and what is expected of the partners that are involved."***
>
> —Bill Tate, Convention Planning Services

with the truth sometimes. Our folks have been known to exaggerate a bit to win a deal, or tell the customer something's done and then quickly cover their tracks to make it so."

Cary: *"You're right. This could be a sticking point with us. Let's talk about how we'll deal with it . . ."*

Feedback: Putting Punch in Your Pacts

Setting up cues is part one of a two-part drill. The other half is actually cueing your partner when the relationship needs improvement. In the words of choreographer Gene Columbus:

> You must always know where you are in relation to all the other dancers. It takes giving and reading cues worked out in advance. This creates a clean and confident movement that is joyful to watch. By the same token, uncertainty is the mark of a poor dance.

A partnership must be based on a living agreement, growing with the business, evolving to accommodate changing conditions and unforeseen circumstances. Feedback means responding to cues and adjusting the performance in real time—while it's under way—when partners feel the partnership is spinning off the stage, changing in ways that conflict with its purposes, goals, and agreements.

There are three moves that can make giving feedback more powerful *and* more fruitful.

1. Create a Climate of Identification

Your first objective is to enhance your partner's receptivity to feedback by showing that you identify with your partner. Start with comments that have an "I'm like you—that is, not perfect" kind of message. Telegraph your empathy, respect, and admiration. Partners can hear even the strongest feedback if it is delivered with concern and compassion.

2. State the Rationale for Feedback

Effective feedback is given in context, not out of the blue. When you hear feedback and end up thinking, "Where did that come from?" or "Why are you telling me this?" you've probably been given context-free feedback. The issue is not subtlety or diplomacy; it is understanding. Help your partner gain a clear sense of why the feedback is being given.

3. Act Like You're Giving Yourself the Feedback

Although feedback is best heard when delivered with sensitivity, it must also be clear. It's important that the one receiving the feedback doesn't walk away wondering, "What did my partner not tell me that I need to hear?" Deliver feedback the way you'd like to receive it yourself.

Rehearsing in Action: Giving Feedback

Dale: *"Wow, what a great meeting! Your people are really creative."*

Cary: *"Thanks! But I'll be honest—your associates keep us on our toes. Our operations director was telling me the other day it's been years since he's been this challenged."*

Dale: *"That's good to hear. Speaking of creativity, I can tell how important innovative thinking is to you—and I respect that a lot!"*

Cary: *"You bet! I want our organization to stay on the cutting edge."*

Dale: *"Because creativity is so important to you—and key to our work together—I have some feedback about your style in meetings."*

Cary: *"Well, we agreed to be straight with each other, so lay it on me!"*

Dale: *"Okay. Now, I could be off base on this, but your facial expressions sometimes give a critical message. When we were freewheeling, you looked kind of pained, like someone had said something wrong. I think some of my people might have gotten the wrong message. Am I being clear?"*

Cary: *"You bet! And I'm glad you told me. I can see how my being too quick to judge an idea might stop someone from being spontaneous with ideas—especially if that person is new and doesn't know me that well."*

Finding the Dance Teacher in Your Partner

Giving feedback is just part of the task. The other is to get your partner to give you feedback, to become your mentor—your dance teacher. "Growing together is the secret to making partnerships mature and last," says Sharon Decker, Lynnwood Foundation president. "By working together," reports Ted Townsend, president of Townsend Engineering Company, "both businesses and profits grow in a way competitors have a hard time matching. It is each partner teaching the other what one knows that the other doesn't. Partners benefit and the partnership thrives."

Before asking for feedback, volunteer a brief, honest summary of areas in which you know you need to improve. This tells your partner you are seriously interested in input and not just fishing for compliments. When your partner tries to offer candid critique, assertively thank your partner. "That's very helpful. Tell me more about that" can go a long way toward encouraging the mentor in your partner.

Give your undivided attention during all partner feedback. Avoid any hint of defensiveness; don't interrupt to explain your actions. Prime the pump by bringing up something about yourself that you know frustrates your partner: "I know it sometimes bothers you when I . . . What else do I do that bugs you?"

Rehearsing in Action: Tell Me More

Cary: *. . . I can see how my being too quick to judge an idea might stop someone from being spontaneous with ideas—especially if that person is new and doesn't know me that well. I also know I sometimes come across as domineering, especially when a meeting goes off in a direction I didn't expect. Tell me more. What else do you see me do that you think stops people from being creative?"*

Dale: *"Well, now I think you're being a bit too hard on yourself. With the confident crew you have, I'm not sure you really stop anyone from saying what he thinks. I do think that sometimes you may slow them down. And sometimes your control is important when the group needs leadership. But you might work at not being quite so quick to give your opinion. I have to work on the same habit—slowing down my reactions—so they have a chance to give their ideas and views."*

Cary: *"That's helpful. I'll work on those points. And I appreciate your feedback. Keep calling me on stuff like that."*

Dale: *"I will—but only if you promise to return the favor."*

Great partnerships are exercises in loyalty. And loyal partners go the distance. They endure because they care and because they can. The "care" side comes from deep allegiance to their relationship and to their partner. The "can" side is all about "being in shape." Great dancers can dance and dance, long past fatigue, pain, and distraction, because they have conditioned themselves for adversity. Great partnerships can keep going and going for the same reason.

Conditioning in the dance world is a combination of stretching, repetition, and drill. In the world of partnering, conditioning involves clarifying goals, agreeing on cues, and giving and getting feedback. Dances are rehearsed on the stage or dance floor; the platform for partnership rehearsal is a standard set of protocols that leads to partnership greatness. In the next lesson we will explore these building blocks of great partnerships in depth.

LESSON

Blocking Out Your Performance Together

7

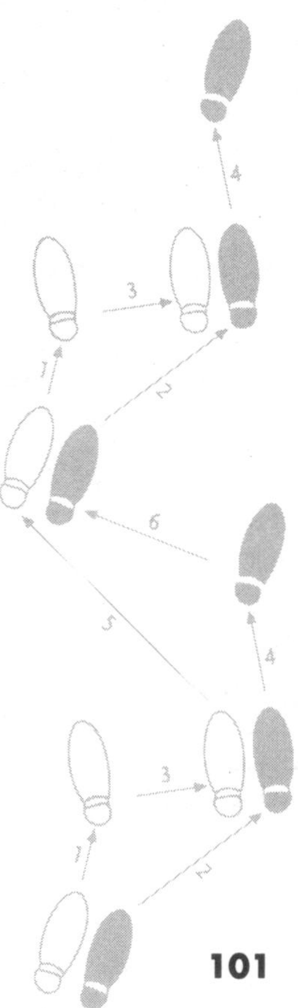

AS THE REHEARSAL PROCEEDS, THE TIME ARRIVES FOR THE dancers to try out their moves. First, the rules are discussed; everyone gets a chance to review them and suggest changes before they are finished. Once everyone agrees and understands, the dancers begin moving about according to these rules. As the moves grow more and more familiar and instinctive, the creative instinct takes over, and the dance takes wings.

Partnership Protocols: The Bedrock Basics

All performances are based on a set of protocols—the principles, truths, conventions, and rules honored by those who engage in the effort. In poker, everyone agrees that a full house is a pair plus three of a kind. Writers in the English language accept that "alphabetical order" means A, followed by B, followed by C, and so forth. Basketball players never argue about how many points they get for a free throw from the foul line.

In dance, the mechanics of how and where on the stage the dancers will perform is known as *blocking*. Dancers walk through the steps so each gets a clear picture of his or her relationship to the other dancers, the props, and the score. Blocking is not concerned with mood or expression; it's about basic moves and familiarity with the environment.

Setting up the protocols for a partnership is like blocking a dance. Wise partners ensure that they share the same picture of their operating rules and environment—where each will go, what each will do, how much of the stage the joint effort will cover. Partnership protocols are the mutually agreeable absolutes that serve as a foundation for trust, confidence, and communication.

> ***"We are constantly asking ourselves, 'Are we doing business at the level we want to? Are we worthy of this partnership?' And we want partnerships with people who ask themselves those same questions."***
>
> **—Terry McElroy, McLane Company**

As we described in lesson 1, when we studied the transcripts of our interviews with people who have experienced great partnerships, we were intrigued by the similar "truths" they described. The more we probed, the more we realized there was a universal set of six bedrock basics. Honoring these truths ensures longevity and productivity; ignoring them risks the demise of the partnership. We discovered that, although the performance goals of a partnership may be unique and the agreements customized, the "etiquette" of great partnerships never changed.

We challenge you to examine the greatest, longest-lasting partnerships you've enjoyed. We believe you'll find that they are based on the following six principles, honored willingly and confidently by all partners.

Expect the Best

This principle sounds like one of those overworked truisms used to whip up morale in faltering organizations—but it has many meanings. Among them are that great partners *go into* relationships with expectations. They don't go into a partnership with a "What the heck, let's see what happens" attitude.

Great partners are rarely people who are habitually suspicious or pessimistic. Nor are they naive about the failings of others. Instead, they are both optimistic and pragmatic. They go forward with confidence and trust, expecting others to deal honorably with them and put forth their best effort. They have a clear idea of what the relationship ought to be like, they let their partners know their expectations, and they stay alert to problems. They also know that defects can be repaired by the force of their will and the power of the relationship.

Great partners know that they are not perfect, nor do they expect anyone else to be perfect. But they have faith that they can become better and that their partners and others they deal with share their desire. Belief becomes truth because the energy of the partnership wills it. While hope springs eternal in life, it leaps barriers and vaults doubt in great partnerships.

> ***"Our best partnerships are about leveraging our resources. They are a product of everyone working hard to make the most of what we can pool together. And sometimes we even have fun."***
>
> **—Robbie Smith, U.S. Department of Energy**

Be All, There

We asked a wise philosopher to tell us what she noticed about successful partnerships. "They're shiny," she replied with a smile. "They glow in the dark." We had interviewed her early in our research, so we were puzzled by her assessment. Later, as we listened to great partners describe their great partnerships in action, we came to understand what she meant. Great partnerships are "on."

> ***"You're dancing when you are real enthused about talking with your partner."***
>
> **—Ed Novak, Broker Restaurants**

Partnerships work best when they're wide awake. Great partnerships have a perpetual energy and intensity in every encounter. Great parnters are never lazy or indifferent; when they are there, they are *all* there. In conversations, they are attentive—showing curiosity when they listen, animation when they contribute.

"Partners must be willing to move mountains for each other," advises Producers Livestock Association's Dennis Bolling. "If no is the likely answer, good partners must be willing to add, 'but give me a little time and I'll think about how we can.'" Does this mean great partners never rest? Of course not. When they cannot be all there, they serve notice. Their continuous energy is fueled by a need to squeeze the most from every important moment.

Assert the Truth

Ask anybody what he or she believes to be the number one cause of divorce. After a few cute answers—like "marriage"—eight in ten will tell you "communication." A key protocol for partnership is straight talk, a two-way pursuit of the truth. An absence of candor reflects the decline of trust and the deterioration of the relationship.

No partnership is likely to be perfect all the time, but when problems occur, the healthy partnership, like the healthy marriage, is marked by candor and acceptance of criticism. Honesty fuels more honesty if defensiveness is absent. And as candor triggers improvement, those who serve feel responsive, those served feel heard, and the partnership feels healthy.

"Partnership success takes communication that results in clear understanding," says Jack Tester of Contractors 2000. "This means total and complete understanding." "One partner may be more competent than the other," adds Dennis Bolling, "but each must know what the other is doing. Both must be absolutely clear on the next move. In fact, like world-class basketball players [or dancers], great partners can feel the other's next move."

Honor Your Partner

Honor is made of admiration and respect. When we honor people, it means we admire who they are or what they do—attributes that have nothing to do with us.

With a partner, however, we tend to feel personally involved. We may admire and respect a partner but feel possessive or overprotective about the person and the relationship. This may make the partner at first feel secure and valued; eventually, however, possessiveness may be perceived as suspicion or mistrust. The relationship will cease to grow.

Great partners honor their partners by giving them room to be the best they can be—different, special, unique. "Bottom line, partnership is love," says Michael Metzler of Metzler & Company. "It is a relationship in which I will go to any extent (within reason) to support you. It may take time, it may take money, but you do what it takes." Ed Novak of Broker Restaurants expresses a similar sentiment: "It requires real open and public support—almost as a form of love for the other."

Keep Your Promises

Trust is the glue of partnerships, and reliability is the main ingredient of trust. A partner who can be relied on to keep promises is a partner who believes in protecting the sacredness of commitment. "Partnerships live or die by promises kept," says Marcia Corbett of AchieveGlobal.

Keeping agreements, according to Gay Hendricks and Kate Ludeman in their book *The Corporate Mystic*, is

> joining forces with the creative powers of the universe, the same power that makes oak trees where no trees were before. Having stepped into unity with the creative force in the universe, you need to make good on the creation or cancel it out cleanly. Otherwise, you are bucking the greatest power there is.

Promises are covenants of assurance. Promises kept give relationships security in the way honor gives it adventure.

> ***"It's when you get referrals, schedules are kept, phone calls returned promptly, they make suggestions for improvements, a sense of caring is ever present, and your meetings are engaging."***
>
> —Syd Kershaw, Parker Hannifin

> ***"Reliability is the foundation of mutual trust. It is being able to meet every promise every time."***
>
> —Carlo Medici, Covance

Stay . . . on Purpose

The protocol "Stay . . . on purpose" has an intentional double meaning. "Stay" reminds us that a partnership requires resolve and tenacity to stay "on purpose"—that is, focused on its goals. "Partnerships take passion!" says Kevin Freiberg of the San Diego Consulting Group. Passion comes from shared purpose or collective vision. Purpose lends partnership its optimism, its magic, its reason for being.

The "on purpose" side of the protocol also reminds us that healthy partnerships are intentional or deliberate. They require commitment, whether the going is rocky or smooth, a dogged determination to stay the course and keep the partnership working. Partners with faith in a shared vision must rely on the relationship to realize that vision.

Take Your Mark!

Once you and your partner have agreed on the goals of the partnership, developed clear cues, and established the protocols of your dance together, you're ready to practice or "act out" the thornier parts of your partnership agreements. Gene Columbus puts it this way: "When dancers 'get to their mark,' it is more than a piece of direction or instruction. It is drilled and drilled—over and over. Choreography doesn't make a dance great, practice does."

There are many ways to approach reality practice. Below, we've outlined three—behavior rehearsal (sometimes called role play), exaggeration, and fantasy work.

Behavior Rehearsal

Effective behavior rehearsal requires solid and careful preparation to enhance learning. Start by identifying an interpersonal skill or behavior you want to try out together. The key is to be clear and specific about the partnership dilemma to be overcome. "To handle a major disagreement over a value difference involving quality assurance" is a much better defined target than "to improve our approach to conflict resolution."

Next, identify the context in which the hypothetical problem occurs. How do you tell a partner that the partnership must come to an end? If the partnership has been effective and enjoyable, the answer will be quite different than if you're bringing an end to an unpleasant or unproductive relationship. To make it realistic, both parties in the rehearsal must be aware of the real-life conditions that are likely to surround the problem.

Once you and your partner have agreed on the skills to be rehearsed and their context, outline the behaviors to be practiced. What actions would be most likely to result in excellence? Try to get a clear understanding your partner's needs. State your own needs. Be up front with one another about vulnerabilities and distracting tendencies in situations like the one you are working on. Remember: this is not a test to demonstrate incompetence or humiliate your partner, it's an exercise designed to identify areas for understanding.

Keep in mind also that this is not play acting or theater; it is people trying out behaviors similar to those they plan to use in the partnership. The purpose of the "dress rehearsal" is not to learn a script or memorize catchwords or clever phrases for later use. It is to discover traps or likely errors to avoid and to build confidence for "opening night"—the real-life partnership.

Rehearsing in Action: Behavior Rehearsal

Dale: *"I watched how you handled that unexpected visit from your attorney last week when we were meeting. It made me think."*

Cary: *"About what?"*

Dale: *"About what's going to happen when you and I have a serious disagreement and have to duke it out. I'm not looking for a fight, I just know that in any close working relationship, there will be conflict."*

Cary: *"What's that got to do with our attorney?"*

Dale: *"Well . . . Again, I might be way off base here, Cary, but you seemed pretty nervous and anxious. Your attorney seemed to be getting his way with you more than I thought should happen. Maybe we should sort of walk through what might happen if you and I got into a disagreement."*

Cary: *"But talking with you and talking with our attorney are completely different. That's not a relevant example."*

Dale: *"Maybe not, but wouldn't you agree that you're a bit uncomfortable with confrontation?"*

Cary: *"Well, sure, isn't everybody? But if it makes you feel better to see what it's going to be like, I'll be glad to role play it with you."*

Dale: *"I'd appreciate it. I think you might find it helpful, too. Why don't we try this: let's pretend you've just discovered what you think is a deliberate attempt to sabotage your efforts with a customer we both know. You walk into my office, assuming I either master-minded or participated in the deception. To make it realistic, we can pick the Portia deal."*

Cary: *"That's a good choice. I can just be myself on that one. Let's pretend I've just confronted you on the sabotage—the alleged sabotage—and you sit there silently glaring at me."*

Dale: *"Okay, that's good. Let's get into it! What do you say next?"*

Cary: *"You mean, right after 'You dirty, rotten #@%&!?'" (They both laugh.)*

Exaggeration

Great dancers are keenly aware of the stress or pressure points in their dance. They rehearse through exaggeration and overcompensation. A difficult pirouette is rehearsed at double speed, a challenging pinwheel is practiced in slow motion or with weights. The aim is to make calamity child's play by courting its dark side in advance. When a real challenge occurs during a performance, partners are prepared. Their confidence and composure are not shaken by difficulty.

A senior executive in a Midwest bank revealed to the corporate treasurer of a large systems engineering firm that he struggled with a nasty temper, especially when he felt his expertise was being challenged. They were a few weeks into a potentially exciting partnership in the construction of an urban office complex. "I think it goes back to being the youngest in a family of three over-achieving, highly successful children," he admitted. "It is frankly a silly reaction, but I'm usually seething before I know it." The treasurer responded by asking the key rehearsal question: How can we best deal with this in our relationship?

> ***"You have to be able to determine if you can grow together."***
>
> **—Marcia Corbett, AchieveGlobal**

Their solution was to use exaggeration. "I have a suggestion," began the corporate treasurer. "Since you're working on keeping your temper in check and you want feedback, when you go into a fury, I'll grab my chest and fall on the floor like I've been shot. It'll give me some exercise, you'll get immediate feedback, and we'll both get a good laugh!" It worked! After a few theatrical dying scenes, the banker was checking his own wrath; the gimmick could be retired.

Fantasy Work

Fantasy work has just one purpose: to flesh out as many "how do we handle" scenarios as possible around the thornier possibilities in the future life of the partnership. Think of it as a series of thoughtful "what ifs" for reflection and discussion.

One way partners can begin this effort is by independently writing out all the "what ifs" each can identify without regard to the solution. Bring the list to a partner meeting. Take turns reading a "what if," and jointly explore ways that either a partner or the partnership might handle it effectively. That the actual solution might ultimately differ from the imagined solution is not important. The two main goals are to bolster early partnership confidence and to subtly uncover potential problems that might be prevented by early planning.

"Role play some 'what if' scenarios," suggests Tucker Rocky Distributing president Frank Esposito. "State how you expect to be treated. Learn what the other person expects. Put potentially damaging scenarios on the table and openly discuss how you will handle these situations. The more you blue-sky the possibilities and the more you actually talk through how you'd like to handle them, the more you learn about your partner as well as yourself. It makes the relationship much stronger."

Below are few sample "what ifs" to get your discussion started. Add your own. Ask your associates (colleagues, friends, customers, attorney) to suggest others.

- What if one of us develops a long-term disability?
- What if one of us encounters a major, unexpected, time-consuming distraction (divorce, lawsuit, natural disaster)?
- What if one of us gets bored with the partnership?
- What if one or both of us realize that one or both of us are no longer benefiting from the partnership?
- What if one or both of us find another partner better suited to our needs?
- What if one of our organizations is the victim of a hostile takeover?

- What if our customers (or constituents) find our partnership unappealing?

Goals give the partnership a destination. Cues give it signposts. Feedback gives it precision. And protocols give the partnership important grounding. These parameters offer stability and guidance along the path to greatness. In the words of dance great Martha Graham, "Being a dancer was an act of total commitment costing not less than everything."

LESSON

Three Partnering Drills 8

PARTNERSHIPS, LIKE DANCES, NEED REHEARSALS. MISTAKES will inevitably be made in the early stages of any relationship. In a partnership trial performance, mistakes have only one important consequence: growth. A rehearsal brings the most likely mistakes to the attention of all, creating an opportunity to clarify goals, negotiate agreements, and review protocols. A rehearsal is a testing ground for creative interpretation, collaborative discovery, and fine tuning.

Healthy relationships take time for learning and relationship building. Too often, alliances are formed prematurely over a quick cup of coffee and get practiced on the run. Proper relationship building takes quality time. As an entertainment industry client of Heather's puts it:

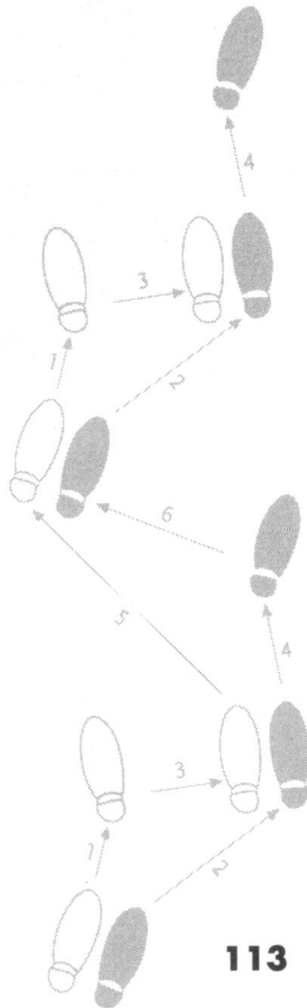

> After you decide you're going to partner, it's important to decide how you will govern or manage the partnership. The really successful partnerships set up the discipline ahead of time—things like what reports do we produce each month, how often do we meet, how do we judge success. . . . Good partnerships are well managed from the start.

Once the decisions are made about what to do, the partnership needs to learn how to do those things well and effectively. This requires the use of relationship tools. We will outline below three of the tools that we have found crucial in practicing the dance of partnership: dramatic listening, productive dialogue, and giving advice.

Keep in mind that these "how to" tools are effective only if the "what to dos" have been agreed upon. If the big picture goals are unclear, if the agreements or cues have not been negotiated, if feedback is not valued, or if you disagree on the bedrock basics, all manner of partnership work will be for naught.

Partnering Drill #1: Dramatic Listening

Most partners *can* be great listeners. Let their eight-year-old come crying about a neighborhood conflict, and you'll see great listening. Zero in on a quiet corner conversation in the funeral home during the wake of a friend, and you'll see great listening.

How do great partners avoid the everyday distractions that get in the way of dedicated listening? Effective listeners don't *start* doing anything special—they just *stop* doing something normal. Dramatic listening has less to do with communication management than with noise management.

Great partners get focused and stay focused. When listening is their goal, they make it *the* priority. When a partner needs you to listen, pretend you just got a gift of five minutes with your greatest hero. Think about it! If you could have only ten minutes with Moses, Mozart, Mother Teresa, or a loved one who has passed away, would there be anything or anyone who could intrude on that precious time?

Listening done well is complete absorption. The mission is to be so crystal clear on the other person's message that it becomes a "copy and paste" command from one brain's computer screen to another's. Perhaps the expression "meeting of the minds" should be changed to "joining of the minds."

When your partner asks, "How would you . . . ?" get her to tell you what she would do before offering your opinion. When your partner voices a frustration or concern, before delivering an answer, try to communicate through your actions that her message got through, especially when the answer is likely to be different from the one she thought she was going to get.

Partnering Drill #2: Productive Dialogue

Think back on the conversations you have had that you most valued. Consider the elements that made those conversations or dialogues positive and productive ones. There were probably several: People who valued each other's view, even if the views were different. All parties participating in the give-and-take, listening to each participant and keeping the dialogue focused. What was the result? Closure. Issues were resolved, understanding was reached, learning occurred. These three components—valuing, give-and-take, and closure—are the basis of fruitful discussions in great partnerships.

Valuing

Valuing begins with a clear, recognizable mindset—the setting of tone that begins a productive discussion. Three simple but powerful questions should be answered; if you and your partner are of one mind on the answers, then the discussion will probably have a positive and productive outcome.

- **Why are we here?** First, both parties need to come together on the purpose of the conversation. A simple statement followed by confirmation is generally sufficient: "Lisa, I see this conversation as an opportunity for the two of us to discuss the best approach for doing the Dickinson project. Is that your view?"
- **What will it mean to you?** The benefits side of mindset is important. Not only does it help focus the exchange, it enhances your partner's motivation. A lethargic, "Here we go again, another conversation with ol' Cliff" beginning can suddenly turn into "Wow, this conversation with Cliff is going to be really helpful!"
- **How shall we talk?** Mindset also includes signaling the tone and style desired. Even if the tone is implied, a brief reminder can be useful in serving notice that open, candid, freewheeling conversation is needed and expected. It also helps clarify the "rules of engagement," paving the way for a no-surprises discussion.

> ***"We know we have a great partnership when we see their problem as our problem."***
>
> **—Hank Payne, Federal Aviation Administration**

Cary: *"Dale, thanks for getting right back to me. This is a good chance for us to decide how we'll handle the press announcement of our new alliance. Does that square with what you see us doing?"*

Dale: *"You bet. This is a perfect time, too. The press release will hit the wire later today, and I'm sure we'll be getting a few calls from the media."*

Cary: *"My thought was that we should spend fifteen minutes or so looking at options and then brainstorm some of the kinds of questions we might get and how we might answer them. I'll be as candid as I can, and I'm counting on you to fill in a lot. You've had a lot more experience with this kind of thing."*

Dale: *"Sounds good to me. After we finish, we might want to bring in each of our marketing directors to review . . ."*

Give-and-Take

"Priming the pump" is an expression as old as the first mechanized water well. Once upon a time most homes had a backyard pump that sometimes had to be primed in order to function. A large pitcher of water was poured in, which, combined with the pumping action of a busy arm, "seeded" water from the ground. The partnership version of priming the pump is the give and take that leads to productive dialogue. There are three good ways to do this: ask clarifying questions, paraphrase (or mirror), and summarize.

Ask clarifying questions. The questions that work best are direct but not leading. Open-ended questions are usually best—questions beginning with "what," "when," "where," or "how." Or use language that asks for an explanation or solution: "Describe your reasons for choosing that approach."

Here are more examples of open-ended questions helpful in clarifying:

- "What do you see as the major liabilities associated with this venture?"
- "How did your group approach the due diligence problem you encountered?"
- "Describe what makes this component important to your organization."

"I now see that what I did in the past was create a situation where whoever was assisting me finally gave up. I didn't know I was not trusting. It's amazing that I was that strong in such a detrimental way in terms of their contribution. I never allowed them to contribute in a way that would have helped me."

—Ron Field, in *Conversations with Choreographers*

Avoid questions that begin with "why." In most cultures the word "why"—when used to start a sentence that ends in a question mark—is easily perceived as judgmental and indicting. Granted, body language can play a role in how such questions are perceived, but even with perfect body language our antennae rise when we hear a "why" question. Find ways to soften the question by seeking an explanation: "Why did you do that?" can sound much harsher than "What were your reasons for doing that?"

Paraphrase or mirror. The goal of paraphrasing is to demonstrate that you understand what is being communicated. Partners appreciate knowing that they have been heard. To use paraphrasing as a mirror of your partner's meaning, punctuate your restatements with a ".", not a "?" or a "!". Make sure your voice turns down, not up.

Paraphrasing also needs to be in your own words. If you simply repeat your partner's, it will have a wooden, apathetic tone.

Dale: *"I just got the numbers from our CFO on the first quarter of our partnership. We cut overhead by 32 percent and increased our margins by 8 percent!"*

Cary: *"The financial results show that the partnership is working."*

Dale: *"And how! If we can figure out the formula we used for measuring carrying costs and seasonally adjust the numbers, I think we ought to consider doing this in other aspects of our business."*

Summarize. Summarizing is similar to paraphrasing, with a slight but significant difference. In paraphrasing, you check for understanding by mirroring the meaning; in summarizing, you synthesize by condensing the meaning of your partner's comments into a sentence or two (or, if the comments were lengthy, into a paragraph) and repeating the synthesized information as a summary. Summarizing typically begins with such phrases as "In other words . . . ," "What you're saying is that . . . ," and "In summary, you think that. . . ."

Closure

Productive dialogues are productive because they lead to an outcome. Stuff happens!

Michael Somers, VP of technical operations at Computer Curriculum Corporation in Sunnyvale, California, describes how his organization's Regional Triangle Partner meetings accomplish closure: "Sales, training and service/installation personnel meet monthly for a healthy dialogue, but always with a 'So what have we agreed to achieve?' discussion at the end." Summarize your partnership discussions with a focus on accountability and results.

Partnering Drill #3: Giving Advice

Giving advice is one of the most important components of effective partnership communications. It can also be one of the most challenging. Recall the last time someone said, "Let me give you a little advice!" No doubt it quickly put you in a defensive posture. Advice giving works only if the intent is support, not criticism, and if the tone conveys permission to *not* take your advice.

There are four moves that can make giving advice more powerful *and* more productive.

1. Clearly State the Issue, Problem, or Goal

Begin your advice giving by being clear with your partner about its focus or intent. Your advice may not be sweet music to your partner's ears, but it's better to keep your thoughts focused and not come on like a scatter-gun. You may be offering advice on a needed improvement, a different approach, or new skill: "Cary, I wanted to talk with you about the fact that the Connellan report we need for the due diligence review was late for the third quarter in a row."

2. Make Sure You Have a "Meeting of the Minds" on the Focus

If you think something is an issue, challenge, or concern, but your partner thinks otherwise, your advice will be viewed as overcontrolling or smothering. Make sure your partner is as eager to improve and learn as you are to see him improve and learn.

You may discover that your partner has already determined what to do and has little need for your advice. Your goal is to hear your partner say something like this: "Dale, I appreciate your mentioning that. I'm concerned about that too."

What do you do if your partner disagrees on the importance of your concern? As Abraham Lincoln said, "A person convinced against his will is of the same opinion still." Take a broader perspective. Be sure to have objective information (as a tool, not as proof) that can be helpful in collectively examining needs, gaps, and requirements. If all else fails, defer the conversation to a time when your partner demonstrates a greater readiness to learn. Never resist resistance!

3. Ask Permission to Give Advice

This is the most important step! Your goal at this point is twofold: (1) to communicate advice without triggering your partner's resistance, and (2) to keep ownership of the improvement opportunity with your partner. This does not mean saying, "May I have your permission to . . . ?" It does mean saying something like "I have some ideas that might be helpful to you." Remember, the goal is to minimize any perception that you're trying to control or coerce your partner.

4. State Your Advice in the First Person Singular

Phrases like "you ought to" quickly raise partner resistance. Keeping your advice in the first person singular—"what I found helpful" or "what's worked for me"—helps eliminate the "shoulds" and "ought tos." Your partner will hear such advice without the internal noise of defensiveness or resistance.

Dale: *"That was one tough meeting! I hope we don't have to have too many of those."*

Cary: *"Me too! I thought Lynn was going to explode. I can't remember ever seeing that much rage in one spot!"*

Dale: *"At least we got through it without bloodshed. You seemed very uptight throughout the whole meeting."*

Cary: *"I was—and I'm sure it was pretty obvious. Meetings like that make me anxious; I can't think too clearly. And I worry about saying the wrong thing and making matters even worse."*

Dale: *"I know what you mean. I've had my share of super-tense meetings. But I've discovered a few tips that have helped me. I'd be glad to run through a few of them, if you think you might want to try them out."*

Cary: *"You bet it would! You told me when we started that handling conflict was going to be my achilles' heel."*

Dale: *"I found that taking deep breaths helps calm me. I also try to slow down—to not feel like I have to provide a super-fast response to whatever comes at me. And I keep telling myself this is not personal, even if it sounds personal. Angry people often are using the person they are yelling at as a punching bag for something that has nothing to do with that person. I also work really hard to be the rational person. If I get emotional, it's like pouring oil on a fire—the other person just gets more hostile."*

Cary: *"That's good advice. I'll try it. Especially if Lynn is the dynamite!"*

The Final Rehearsal Point: Trust

Effective dance rehearsals presuppose a lot. The dance director presumes dancers can dance, know their steps (at least at a rudimentary level), are committed enough to the outcome to work hard on preparation, and respect the importance and virtues of rehearsal. Partnership power has similar presuppositions—skill, commitment, respect for the conditions, and so on. But there's one other presupposition that's vital to partnerships, and that's trust.

Whether clarifying goals, agreeing on pacts, providing feedback, or using effective partnership skills, partners must trust one another. According to Jordan Lewis, in his book *Partnerships for Profit*, "The success of an alliance depends on mutual faith. It's hard to take risks with someone you don't trust. And you can't write agreements about enthusiasm." A covenant of trust can be more critical than a contract of deadlines and deliverables.

Trust in partnership involves far more than dependability and reliability. All trust begins with a risk. With no experience together as a basis for trust, each partner takes a risk. The risk of that first step—offering feedback, providing advice, communicating empathy and understanding—leads to experience. Based on what is learned, the experience gives rise to long-term trust. However, risk implies the potential for mistakes, for errors, and for disappointment. From the cauldron of betrayal emerges the real proof of trust. As a partner, we find out whether our colleague can be trusted by the manner in which he or she recovers from betrayed trust.

Partners do not expect their partners to be perfect. They do expect their partners to care when disappointments occur. In fact, partnerships that have experienced disappointment and had that disappointment effectively managed have deeper commitment and greater loyalty.

The Rules of Rehearsal

Partnering without preparation is like dancing without rehearsal. Not only will the partners end up being misfit, miscued, and mistaken, but also something is likely to get broken in the process.

Partners need a clear picture in their heads of *where* the partnership needs to *go* and *what* the partnership needs to *be.*

Great partnerships practice great etiquette. Remember to

Expect the best	Honor your partner
Assert the truth	Keep your promises
Be all, there	Stay . . . on purpose

Great partnerships use planned feedback (*feed* back) as performance fertilizer.

Great rehearsals are overdone, overstepped, and overreached. The discipline of rehearsal will liberate you on stage.

STEP
Four

DANCE LESSONS

"Dancing happens, dancing is always in the present."

—Peter Martins

DANCING

Keeping the Magic in Motion

"Siamese twins!" whispered the silver-headed, elegantly dressed woman to her friend seated beside her. "They dance like two people who are one." Her colleague nodded with enthusiastic agreement as they watched the two dancers merge, spin, disengage, reemerge in a human blend as harmonious as light with shadow. "They are magic in motion," the friend whispered back.

What is world-class partnering "magic in motion"? It encompasses that state of ecstasy when partners find themselves so completely "in the groove" their ideas blend without stirring. It is a oneness so pure that partners complete each other's sentences and seem able to almost read each other's minds. It is rare, it is distinctive, and it is an unmistakable, exhilarating high.

There are many ways to label this special feeling. Athletes call it "playing over your head," dancers refer to it as being "hot" or "on," artists call it "flow" or being in sync with the muses. We call it "partnership squared"! To the outside observer, it truly is "magic in motion."

MAGICAL ENERGY

Regardless of the label, the feeling is an energetic, sparkly magical current of energy which propels you to your highest levels of excellence. And the output of "partnership squared" is generally the stuff of which broken records, new standards, and bar-raising are made.

"Partnership squared" in action yields a state of tingly exultation and blissful joy. As the president of a prominent Tennessee company said of his great relationship with the CEO of a partnered company: "When [the partnership] hits on all cylinders, it's extraordinary and downright intoxicating. We wish we could memorize the formula for sustaining the flow of this partnership. It is an awesome experience. If the feeling was fine whiskey, I'd not only get to know the bootlegger. Hell, I'd buy the still!"

But where does this state of rapture originate? Is there—as our Tennessee friend implies—a secret formula? Not really. You can't program human relationships like software or cook them up from a recipe like some gourmet dish. Partnerships are always divine relationships in the making. As we've said earlier, they are hopeful pursuits of magic, not efforts valued only at the finale. Just as life comes without instructions, there are no surefire guarantees of partnership perfection if you simply "follow the drill." There are some guideposts, though, that can help lead you toward partnership greatness.

Tapping the Source

Partnership impeccably performed looks like "magic in motion." To spectators on the outside, the flow seems magical. To the participants in the midst of the collaborative current that same flow feels like a spiritual surprise.

The inner workings of partnerships, however, are far from magical. Like a great dance performance, the "show" is an orchestrated demonstration of proficiencies and disposition. Both skill and attitude must work in harmony for a winning presentation. A technically accurate dancer with no showmanship or flair would be as unsuccessful as a bumbling amateur with personality plus.

"Dancing" is our label for the zenith of partnership. The climax of great partnerships is a toe-curling rapture that leaves participants longing for ways to keep it going. Like most magical moments, the pinnacle of great partnership is plenty long on magic but too short on moment. The overriding goal is to sustain the exultation.

Dance greatness is a brilliant combination of heart and head. Sustained distinction requires far more than simply finding the groove and riding it to the end. Enduring eminence transpires through the dancers' balance of soul and smartness . . . and diligence!

Partnership is the same. Partnership greatness is maintained through unrelenting spirit and hardworking logic.

LESSON

9 Using Your Heart to Keep Great Partnerships Great

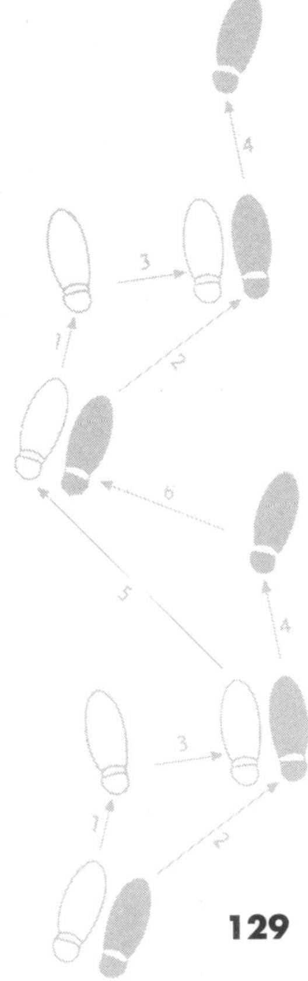

GREATNESS IN DANCING, AS IN PARTNERING, COMES ON ITS own. It can be invited, never imposed; discovered, never invented. It is a spirit that visits partnerships when the stage has been properly set.

There is an ancient Native American ceremony called the "sweat lodge." The goal of a sweat lodge is spiritual cleansing. When it works, participants claim they are visited by a deity in some form—an eagle, a wolf, perhaps a deer. "It doesn't always happen," participants say, "but when it does, it is a great event."

Although the pinnacle of the experience is the surprise visit, much work goes into getting ready. In fact, the process is as important as the outcome. A hut is built. Rocks are chosen, heated red hot, and then placed in a hole dug in the center of the hut. The nearly naked participants sweat, pray, sweat, chant, sweat, and sweat some more. Their ritual creates the stage for the deity to appear, building for the moment when the deity speaks through the medicine man or one of the participants or appears in animal form outside the hut.

If the stage is not properly set, if the participants are not emotionally ready, no visit happens. Even when the participants do everything right, sometimes the deity still does not come. It is a gentle reminder to all that visits are not the result of a formula but the by-product of faith. Disappointed, the participants disperse to try again on another, more fortunate day.

Partnership greatness is like that. You can do your best to create a stage for greatness and still come up short. Greatness is a serendipitous discovery, as much about magic as method. As we interviewed people about their ideas on partnership greatness, we found the same elements mentioned over and over. We offer these elements for your partnership "sweat lodge." We present them as gifts—offerings for you to contribute to help set an inviting stage for a great relationship.

The Gift of Generosity

The noncompetitive nature of an effective partnership means approaching the relationship with a "cast bread upon the water" attitude. Generous partners are unconditional givers, not drivers of hard bargains within the partnership. They give, not because of something they want, but because it is in their nature. Each contribution to the relationship causes it to grow and prosper. The giver mentality creates a legacy of affirmation—it lives on in the language partners use to describe each other and the partnership.

Generosity in some circles might be labeled "love"—sometimes an uneasy word on mahogany row. The late Dr. Clarence Jordan was a brilliant biblical scholar and theologian who translated much of the New Testament into Southern dialect to provide a richer interpretation of the Bible. His crowning contribution was a four-volume work entitled *The Cotton Patch Version of the New Testament*. Jordan's interpretation of a portion of the oft-read First Corinthians 13 says a great deal about generosity.

> Love is long-suffering and kind. Love is not envious, nor does it strut and brag. It does not act up, nor try to get things for itself. It pitches no tantrums, keeps no books on insults or injuries, sees no fun in wickedness, but rejoices when truth prevails. Love is all-embracing, all-trusting, all-hoping, all-enduring. Love never quits.

How do you demonstrate generosity in a partnership? Surprise your partner with a highly personal gift for no particular reason. Remember an important, but not usually celebrated, day in the life of your partner ("I looked it up, this is your anniversary with the company"). In front of someone important to her, give your partner a sincere compliment. Call your partner with a wish for good luck on an upcoming challenge. Use thank-you notes liberally. Send your partner an article on something you remember she's interested in. Remember important days—especially birthdays.

One of the most powerful expressions of devotion is the gift of growth. When you review your partnership with your partner, include a discussion of what you both have learned and what would help you grow even more. Or identify learning experiences that can benefit your partnership and invite your partner to attend with you. When the corporate lending group of Huntington Banks scheduled a customer service training session, for example, each participant invited a key client-partner to attend. Part of the session near the end of the day-long workshop was devoted to a structured activity that enabled lender and client to review their relationship in light of what they had learned together.

The Gift of Faith

Recall a magical moment in your life. Scrutinize it, examine it, dissect it, study it! It may have been catching your first fish or a game-winning pass. It may have been your honeymoon, a super-big business victory, your daughter's graduation, your son's wedding. There was an unexplained magic that elevated the occasion to something greater than the sum of its parts. Callous or cynical people miss the specialness of these moments because they do not believe in the magic.

"Imagine a partnership of three or four people, working together for years. They count on each other. They rely on each other's perspective, talent, wisdom, and skill. They expect one another to be present, physically and mentally. They will not be homogenous thinkers. They will be friends."

—Geoff Bellman, author of *Your Signature Path*

Partnerships work in a similar way. The magic comes to those who believe in it. Partnerships require a clear-eyed view coupled with wide-eyed faith—a leaning-forward, "if we build it they will come" kind of optimism. Great partners rely on a deep-rooted confidence, particularly in trying moments. Partners with faith in the unprovable are open to surprise, innovation, and serendipity.

Faith holders seem happier; they waste less energy worrying about tomorrow or fretting about yesterday. They have confidence in the character of others. Their disappointment at occasionally being snookered pales in comparison with the delight of being surprised by the humanity unleashed by simple acts of trust.

In partnerships, faith can be the superglue that keeps a shaken relationship from shattering. Wise partners are courageous enough to surrender to it, brave enough to trust it. Their innate confidence that their partner will do the right and honorable thing is a leap of faith—not a timid "hop of faith" or an adequate "jump of faith," but a leap of reckless abandon. This prepares the stage upon which surprise can occur.

Like the sweat lodge, when things are right with the universe, stuff happens. As the Archbishop of Canterbury said, "When I pray, miracles happen. When I don't, they don't."

The Gift of Passion

Passion takes the plain vanilla out of encounters and replaces it with magic. In *The Scottish Himalayan Expedition*, W. H. Murray tells us how: "Until one is committed, there is hesitancy, the chance to draw back, always ineffectiveness. The moment one definitely commits oneself, then Providence moves, too. All sorts of things occur to help one that would never otherwise have occurred."

Partnerships need passion. Those who come soaring from the heart spark passion in others. Passion builds a relationship platform that raises everyone to a higher level. People may be instructed by reason, but they are inspired by passion. Think about it. People don't brag about their rational marriages or their reasonable hobbies. You rarely see parents exhibiting "in control" behavior when Junior is rounding third base. And exhortations of ecstasy are never restrained on the fishing bank when the cork suddenly disappears. Yet, somehow, the ardor of "sounds of the heart" is an unwelcome aberration in too many business partnerships.

We have missed the boat on what it means to be a business partner. The business world—the organization—and its partnership situations offer far more predictability than is predictably required. The truth is that rationality oozes from the seams of every business encounter. Partners do not have to add order, sanity, rationality, or logic to their relationship. Every dimension of business life reeks with those qualities. Sane partners foster "insane" passion.

The Gift of Inclusion

"How 'bout going and getting the tractor and parking it in the barn?" These sweet words were music to Chip's ears when he was a ten-year-old growing up on a farm in South Georgia. It was his dad's way of nudging along his maturity. To grant the very special privilege of starting, driving, and parking a large, expensive tractor communicated trust and respect. His gesture also left Chip feeling thrilled—and seven feet tall.

> ***"To dance, put your hand on your heart and listen to the sound of your soul."***
>
> —Eugene "Luigi" Facciuto, *Luigi's Jazz Warm Up*

The parking of the tractor was more than a badge of being "grown up"; it was a symbol of partnership. Chip obviously relied on his dad, but at that moment, his dad trusted him enough to return the honor. Partnership means give-and-take—some level of mutual benefit or reciprocity. If you only serve, you ultimately feel like a slave to your partner. If your partner only gives, the result is the same.

Inclusion is the foundation for consideration and respect. When we take time to thoughtfully involve our partner, we sound a message of commitment. When we defer our solitary, independent needs to a shared experience, we telegraph a sense of respect to our partner.

Inclusion begins by being comfortable enough to ask a partner for assistance. It also means being willing at times to sacrifice a bit on efficiency or effectiveness for the commitment gained by inclusion. It would have been safer and perhaps faster for Chip's dad to have garaged the tractor himself—but instead he opted for partnership over perfection. When you invite a partner to help, the path you take together may not be the one you would have taken alone. The delegator relinquishes control for cooperation.

When you ask your partner for help—or anything else, for that matter—ask only for what is reasonable. And make the request the way your mother taught, with the "may I?" and "please" courtesies we learned growing up. Preface your request with a simple statement—"I need your help"—or a simple question—"May I ask a small favor?" Simplicity and sincerity are important tunes; they help your partner get into the rhythm of partnership. Chip's dad never barked a "go-get-the . . ." kind of order; rather, his "how 'bout" phrasing carried the tone of a partner inviting a partner.

Give your partner a brief background when asking for help. Avoid complaining or whining. Simply, clearly, and positively describe the reason for your request and explain how your partner can assist. Remember that requests for participation must contain the element of choice. Your partner must clearly have an option to pass on involvement; a demand is an invitation for partner resistance. And avoid using guilt as a weapon to compel assistance.

Help your partner see participation as a collective effort. Your partner must see you sharing in the effort or he will feel duped, set up, and unfairly used. Partner participation is a powerful tool for partner commitment. However, remember that the pronoun in power is "we." One last thing. Never forget to express your gratitude.

"No one can talk about great partnering without talking about inclusion and communication," says Bunnie (Patricia) Holman, co-chairman of WYNCOM.

> Our biggest challenge is that we have teams out on the road and 100 people in three buildings. Our business cornerstone is *Lessons in Leadership.* Through colleges and universities around the world, we provide a speaker series with names like Stephen Covey, Tom Peters, and Ken Blanchard. How we maintain our internal partnerships is a major challenge.
>
> We started a practice called "Greetings to Fellows." All program coordinators carry video cameras. They shoot random happenings at the events and tape testimonials. We may go to the same location fifty times, but each event is unique for that speech and audience. These coordinators shoot the glamorous and the trouble spots—like a table collapsing one week, or tickets that did not specify

"Partnerships require a big time investment. You must be proactive and not take the relationship for granted. Since so many things can undermine its effectiveness, limit the number of partnerships you have so you can invest the time and have the patience to grow the ones you have."

—Terry McElroy, McLane Company

room locations. Every Friday, the road crew and the home office crews review the videos together. We learn, we get suggestions, and everyone stays connected. It keeps us all sharp and at our best.

Announcements are made in the offices, over the PA system, when a program is up and running. Those people know they will be able to see for themselves how it went. They hear firsthand what our partners and the universities think. They hear from participants. We keep our partnerships strong by going the extra mile to include and communicate.

A great partnership takes on a life of its own—people together pursuing their dreams, blending their talents and resources. It is more than win-win, more than good synergy. It is the greatness of pure magic.

LESSON

Using Your Head to Keep Great Partnerships Great

10

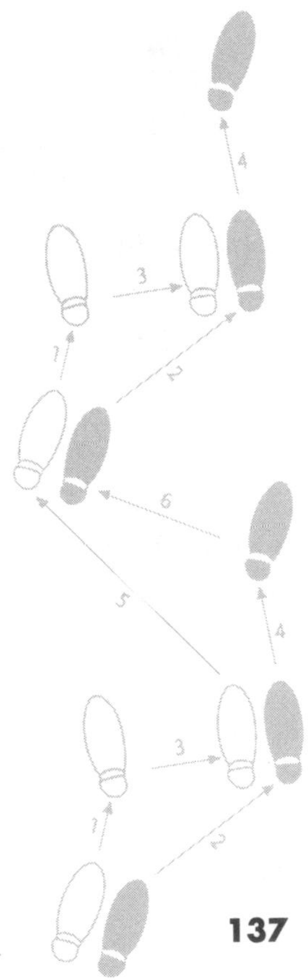

EXTRAORDINARY DANCE AND GREAT PARTNERSHIPS ARE MORE than passion and purpose, covenant and commitment. Greatness is also the product of method and discipline, process and action. If we use only our heads, we cost the dance its richness. However, if we use only our hearts, we cheat the dance of relevance. Great dancers and great partners use their heads wisely.

Partnership greatness depends on rational discipline. Just as solid marriages require more than devotion, partnerships need the toil of focused action and the rigor of considerate attention. The following checklist of partner-initiated practices can help you sustain a great relationship.

Headsmart Tips for Partnership Greatness

- Be the one who initiates email or phone calls, especially upbeat ones; don't just return email or calls after your partner has called.
- Go see your partner in person, don't just call; call, don't just write.
- Be known for your ideas and recommendations, not your defenses and justifications.
- Use straight, candid language. Save diplomacy for the press conference.
- Until shown otherwise, assume that your partner's actions and intentions are honorable.
- Use problem-solving "we" language, not judgmental "you owe me" language.
- Litter your meetings with a lot of discussion about what you (plural) are doing right, rather than dwelling solely on what you are doing wrong.
- Keep differences and conflict in the open, never hidden. Uncover and discuss interpersonal tension as soon as you feel it.
- Never badmouth your partner. Defend your partner when others criticize, unless you have overwhelming evidence to the contrary. Then let the others do the talking.
- Focus on "our collective future," not a rehash of the pains or debts of the past.

"Partners must affirm partners. Partnerships take constant attention and hard work. Without affirmation, you risk taking each other for granted. As a partnership gets more automatic and mature, the more crucial affirmation becomes."

—Kevin Freiberg,
San Diego Consulting Group

- Rather than automatically shifting blame to your partner, accept responsibility until the two of you can work out where it belongs.
- Approach problems as opportunities and errors as teaching tools. Celebrate excellence, not just results.
- Praise without criticizing—no "yes, but's." Be long on affirmation, short on correction. Correct to improve, never to prove.
- Be clear but succinct in your partnership communications. Long-winded communications can waste time and sap energy.
- Assume there will be problems and work out ways to deal with them before they occur. The emergency, fire-fighting approach can strip partnership of vitality and trust.

"Good partnerships need continual maintenance and occasional calibration. Like a finely tuned vehicle, if you're going to run it hard every day and depend on it so intensely, you must treat it well. My advice is regular checkup meetings and strict communications, to make sure everyone in the relationship is 'calibrated.'"

—Michael Somers, Computer Curriculum Corporation

Getting Support from Others

There is a classic competitive dance called the quick step. The masters of this exciting dance are able to combine a waltzlike grace from the waist up with extraordinarily fast footwork from the waist down. The effect is the same as being able to watch, first above and then below the surface, a duck swimming up a stream. The visible "above water" grace can fool the audience into thinking that the part they cannot see is functioning smoothly and quietly also. Partners who keep their trials and tragedies beneath the surface can be inadvertently denied the external support they may need.

A great dance is rarely performed in an empty hall. The power of a dance partnership is always influenced by factors on stage, or backstage, or in the audience. Great dancers rely on the resources of their environment. Stagehands can be as important to gaining encores as the right score.

All partnerships risk becoming so inner focused they miss important signals that could improve their performance. Sometimes important people who are witnesses to the partnership or are indirectly affected by the partnership can provide early warnings, valuable cues, and useful suggestions, all aimed at partnership enhancement.

> ***"Feel from the inside. Don't be distracted by externals. Don't do anything that hurts. Don't pretend. Don't do anything faster than you want. Watch it, feel it, then move."***
>
> —Eugene "Luigi" Facciuto, *Luigi's Jazz Warm Up*

"It was the security officer we contracted who first warned us we were on the road to disaster," said an executive of his near-exit experience with a key vendor-alliance. "The security officer came to me one day and mentioned that George was not the friendly guy he had been a couple of months earlier when we started working together. He put it this way: 'When I worked the reception desk in the building, Mr. Smith was all smiles. But when I worked the security gate checking cars in and out of the visitors' parking lot, he left looking all mad.'" The early warning led to an open discussion that revealed major unspoken dissatisfactions.

Seek the input of anyone who touches your partnership. Make a list of the many people who might offer insight, feedback, or suggestions—vendors, attorneys, customers, support staff, contract staff, family, your partner's assistant. If you make a point of frequently pursuing input, feedback, and suggestions, you are creating an important invitation for unsolicited support. Impromptu input like the security officer's can be the most valuable, but quality input generally requires laying groundwork.

Finally, heed an important warning: spectators and stagehands are not the partnership. Get input, value it, consider it, but not to the exclusion of your own view. Only you and your partner know the goals, cues, agreements, and protocols that govern your partnership performance. Remember the adage: "Those who cannot hear the music think the dancers are mad!"

Marketplace madness is contagious. It is easy to get sidetracked by frivolous fads or impulsive whims. Great dancers are always in touch with their audience, yet they never lose touch with the reason they are on stage. Great partnerships stay far from the madding crowd and mercurial spectators by staying focused on the partnership's purpose and goal. As distractions surface, they exhibit grace under pressure. Their periodic partnership checkups and their constant communication enable them to look smartly forward without having to look suspiciously backward.

The Dazzle of Dancing

Dancing is giving . . . generous partners take long strides.

Dancing is believing . . . trusting partners work their feet instead of wringing their hands.

Dancing is including . . . participative partners keep the curtains open.

Dancing is soaring . . . passionate partners get all the encores.

STEP

Five

DANCE LESSONS

"A dancer who fears work and failure should get out immediately. It is extremely hard work. If you don't take joy in it, if you're not inspired by it, it is not for you."

—Agnes de Mille

HURTING

Managing the Pain in Partnership

"He's hurt!" whispered the stagehand to one of the wardrobe assistants passing through stage left. They peered from the side stage to watch two world-class ballet dancers entangled in a complex turn on the brightly lit stage. As the injured dancer turned his back to the audience, a tiny tear began to gather in the corner of his eye; his lower lip quivered slightly. When he turned back to the audience, he had masked his pain with a steely will and a confident composure. No one beyond the orchestra pit could have had a clue that he had torn a ligament in his right foot.

"What should we do?" the wardrobe assistant asked the stagehand. They continued to watch, awed by the dancer's endurance and strength. There were still three minutes left to curtains. "Don't worry," said the stagehand with an all-knowing air. "He will signal her, and they'll finish the dance." As if following precisely the stagehand's whispered prescription, the injured dancer gave his partner a private look. Their balance shifted, their turns slightly altered, and she supported his weight. Backstage, after their third triumphant curtain call, he grimaced in pain and she collapsed exhausted into his arms.

Partnerships, like dances, are never pain free. Talk to the participants in any successful partnership and you will hear phrases like "We had our trying moments" or "It was touch and go at times." Some relationships wilt under the agony of despair; some are strengthened by adversity and endure the pain. Some, like the ballet dancers in our opening scene, rely on their relationship while digging down deep for inner strength.

Disappointments are a part of all partnerships! In marriages, failing health can rob capacities, life savings, and long-planned-for retirements. In families, earnest and well-meaning parents are heartbroken by their teenager who rebels in embarrassing ways. Professional dancers and successful partnerships learn to weather disappointments in ways that reflect their resilience, ego strength, and commitment to the long term. Any partnership without occasional pain is a partnership missing opportunities for necessary growth. Pain-free partnerships are not normal.

THE PATHS OF PAIN

Pain can be a path to distinction or signal a rocky time ahead. It can be a crucial hint of deeper, unresolved issues which, if left unresolved, could lead to partnership dissolution. Pain is very often a forewarning of misery in the making, a not-so-gentle tap on the partnership's shoulder.

The first step from pain to partnership greatness is to feel the tap. This requires keeping a "get better" orientation at all times. Never assume the partnership is working at its optimal level. While this is not intended to imply a pessimist view, it is to urge you to place enormous emphasis on keeping your partnership evergreen. Partnerships should always be uneasy connections, never glued down tight. Healthy partnerships move around a lot, but they dance on the solid platform built in the early steps of the relationship. "Slippery stages were the terror of my life," said the great Fred Astaire.

Pain is the natural byproduct of partnership growth. It can even be the prerequisite for great joy, like the bittersweet act of childbirth. Growing pains are byproducts of any partnership in transition. Like the sudden empty-nested feeling parents experience when their youngest departs to college, this discomfort is natural; welcome it as the signal for an invigorating passage ahead.

Sometimes the pain in partnerships is short, but usually it goes on for a while. You need to "know when to hold 'em and know when to fold 'em"—you hold onto pain in your partnership when you believe you can still learn from it. After major surgery on both legs and a very long painful rehabilitation process, Heather learned that one of pain's greatest lessons was patience—as the saying goes, "Time is God's gift so that everything doesn't happen at the same time."

Another important lesson from pain is that you learn who your friends really are. When your partnerships have problems, look to see who is really there for you. Pain also helps you better understand your own strengths and develop new skills to get through the trying times.

Adversity Quotient author Paul Stoltz has said that it is no longer your I.Q. or E.Q. that is the key to achieving success; it is your A.Q. "The pain of conflict," says Jane

Anderson of Saint Vincent Health System, "helps forge a great partnership. As conflicts are resolved, the partnership is strengthened."

Nothing ventured, nothing gained. No pain, no gain. Prepare for the pain and profit from the process.

USING PAIN AS YOUR SIGNAL

How do you know if the pain you experience is a natural growing pain or some less desirable form? Using pain as your signal has two sides: seeing the signal and choosing the right action. Some signals are quietly subtle; some are crudely obtrusive. When pain blinds you with its intensity, it is impossible to ignore. If your partner breaks an important promise, betrays your confidence and shares proprietary information to your competitor, or flatly lies to your face, you are looking at a beacon, not a hint. These much-too-bright-to-ignore signs can bring a partnership to a screeching halt. But these are not the signals that are most challenging to partnerships. Too often we "run the red lights" in our relationships because we are completely blind to their presence.

Finding the Front Edge

How do you spot the front edge of subtle pain? How do you segregate heart hurts from an array of assorted afflictions with similar symptoms? Might that queasy feeling in your gut just be last night's enchilada? Maybe. But aches of the heart are unique. With the right perspective, they can be sorted from all other ailments.

First, look inward. Reflect on the current state of your partnership. What emotion surfaces as your mind skims across the then-till-now history of your partnership? Focus on your feelings. Do you feel guilty? We do not mean the you-did-something-wicked kind of guilt. Partnership guilt feels more like the tightness in your throat, the hollowness in your gut, and the dread in your heart when you're out of town on your significant other's birthday and forget to call.

Partnership pain can be an uneasy feeling that things are not right with the world. You may detect a slightly depressing sense of loss when you think about the partnership. The relationship may now feel hollow, like you have suddenly noticed that something that used to be there has been taken away and you are worried it may never be replaced. It may even be keeping you up at night.

Once you have looked inward, look outward. Does your partnership communication have a tired, wooden, not totally authentic feeling? Does your dialogue sound robotic, like the chitchat on the last night of a twenty-week road show or the last hour in the booth at a five-day national convention? If you imagine your relationship is a lamp with a rheostat, does it feel like the knob has been turned too far to the left, down to the space between dark and "I think I need to get my eyes checked"? You are looking at the front edge of pain.

Stop, Seize, or Scrutinize

Recognizing pain is the first step. The other side to using pain as a signal is choosing the appropriate action to take. Over the next three lessons, we will focus on three options for pain management:

1. Stop,
2. Seize, and
3. Scrutinize.

Stopping the suffering is the suitable strategy for the pain that has "Destination: Damage" written all over it. Feeling hurt and being injured are two entirely different things; no one gains from the pain of injury. But if the likely outcome looks to be positive growth, the appropriate approach is to "seize." If the pain hurts, but its origins or results are unknown—or it's too early to tell—we recommend you "scrutinize."

One final point. With all the potentially friendly sides of partnership pain, it's important to keep in mind that pain as a perpetual state is to be avoided. *Enjoying pain is not healthy.* If you are in a partnership with someone who seems to thrive on misery, beware. If you find yourself looking for reasons to feel uneasy, wake up!

Masochism in a partnership has many undesirable side effects. First, it creates victims of the people associated with the partnership, who, caught in your whirlpool of hurt, are themselves diminished by it. Second, perpetual pain produces stationary strain. Growth is stymied; creativity is curtailed.

Worst of all, taking pleasure in pain produces miscues in a relationship. We think we have learned how to relate and then are suddenly in a relationship where the signals mean something different. Right is suddenly left . . . or wrong . . . or something. This crisscrossed meta-signaling winds up in misunderstanding and unnecessary conflicts.

Pain can be experienced at many levels, from an uncomfortable pinch to agonizing misery. Like great dance teams, the great partnerships in business and life are those that understand discomfort, know how to manage disappointment, and are able parlay pain's meaningful lessons into master-making strengths. They are able to do what Fred Astaire often sang: "I pick myself up, dust myself off, and start all over again."

Pain requires the capacity to observe, experience, reflect, and adjust—all with improvement in mind. Learning from pain takes an openness to critique from a partner and to feedback from the partnership environment as well as the ability to critique yourself without guilt.

LESSON

What to Do When You Trip Up

11

WE SHOULD POINT OUT SOMETHING THAT YOU HAVE probably already surmised: we do not mean to imply that in a great partnership great equals perfect. In fact, imperfections are what make great partnerships dynamic. To err is human, and so are curiosity, creativity, discovery, growth, strength, and confidence. Mistakes are the events that make us learn and grow.

The dark side of our imperfections, of course, is that sometimes they destroy. They can, and often do, bring a happy, productive partnership to a bitter end. Some onstage stumbles can be worked out in rehearsal or smoothed over in later performances, but an egregious collision resulting in permanent injury can bring down the curtain long before the choreographed end of the dance.

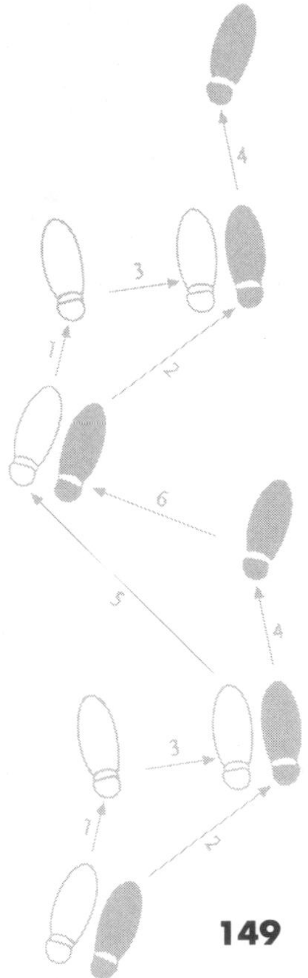

Dance directors often coach novice dancers paralyzed by anxiety onstage to "attack your fear." This is the dark magic found in most resilient relationships: great partners recognize their own fear and guilt and use them as sources of strength and growth. They turn human failings into collaborative virtues.

This lesson outlines some of the common mistakes individuals make in partnerships, along with how they can be overcome. Here is a useful thing to remember: many stumbles in partnerships happen in slow motion. They creep up on you slowly, often with little warning. When you find yourself stumbling, it often means you tripped a good ways back. On the other hand, your partner and constituents may see your mistake when it happens—in time to catch you before you fall flat on your face. A great partner gives early warning and is there to help you recover.

Stumble #1: You Make a Mistake

Mistakes are a part of all relationships—with spouses, friends, and business partners. However, even a false step as serious as betrayed trust can be transformed into renewed partnership commitment when effectively managed. Great partners view partnership recovery as an opportunity to heal a broken relationship.

Here are four moves we have found effective in recovering from the pain that you've caused.

Show Your Humility

Healing communication begins with humility—an expression of authenticity. Speak for yourself, not your unit or company. Apologize in the first person singular—"I'm sorry"—not "All of us in the operations group are sorry." Let your partner witness your genuine concern. Look your partner in the eye. Be forthright and direct. Things went wrong; your partner was disappointed. Acknowledge it honestly and frankly, and be ready to learn from it and move on.

Express Sincere Empathy

Healing communication includes expressions of sincere empathy—words and actions that let your partner know how much you appreciate his pain and predicament. It does *not* mean you must wallow in bad feelings. Empathy communicates understanding and identification. Show that you care. Understanding your partner's concerns from his point of view will only enhance your own understanding of the partnership.

Exhibit Strength and Agility

Healing communication also includes showing strength and agility—words and actions that tell your partner she is dealing with someone who has what it takes to correct the problem. Partners want can-do competence, attentive urgency, and a take-charge, "I'll turn this around" attitude. Any temporary loss of confidence can be overcome if your partner observes your potency and nimbleness in problem resolution. Remember, confidence is restored by what you do, not by what you promise.

Demonstrate Loyalty to the Partnership

Healing communication includes expressions of loyalty—the after-the-fact experiences of your partner that say, "I will not abandon you now that I have regained, I hope, your confidence in our relationship." It is the opposite of taking for granted. It is about continuous care and frequent follow-up. Pick up the phone and call your partner later to find out if everything is back to normal. Send your partner a note. If your partner knows you remember and are still concerned, he will come to realize that the bad experience was an exception.

Stumble #2: You Fear Failure—or Success

Fear strips partnerships of their vitality. It leads to the kind of timidity that holds relationships back from important discoveries and rich depth. There are two main types: fear of failure and fear of success.

Fear of failure often comes from bad history. Failure-fearing partners sometimes have memories of past relationships that caused pain. Wishing to avoid a recurrence, they armor their emotions. They spend a lot of energy keeping the armor in place, energy that would be much better spent on developing trust, taking risks, and tapping their courage.

Sometimes our fear of failure is exceeded only by our fear of success. At first blush, fearing something as positive as accomplishment might seem incomprehensible. Yet, as counter-intuitive as it seems, partnerships falter as often because of partner preoccupation with success as they do because of fear of failure.

Fear of success is grounded in a belief of unworthiness. It begins with the assumption that success comes from a capricious Lady Luck or the fickle finger of fate—as serendipitously as it comes, it can as unexpectedly disappear. Partners sometimes feel they do not deserve success. Old childhood tapes of irrational beliefs (rational from a child's perspective, erroneous for an adult) play loudly in the mind's ear of such partners. They stop themselves short of greatness.

Fear of failure and fear of success both require a "seize" strategy, not a stop tactic. Attack the feeling in much the same way you try to break through a bad mood. Give yourself positive, "you deserve the best" messages—we call it "getting in the spirit of greatness."

Feeling a fear of failure or fear of success can be a healthy sign of growth, if properly managed. The secret is to not back away, but to "suffer and seize." Attack these feelings vigorously. As Tom Peters says, "If you're going to fail, fail forward!" Surround yourself with affirming people, places, messages, and experiences. If you fear failure, catalog your strengths. Talk to people who will affirm your talents. If you fear success, remember how hard you worked to get here—you deserve it.

Stumble #3: You Trip on Your Own Guilt

It happens in every relationship: despite your best efforts, you blow it. A promised report is forgotten, your careless performance of a task hurts the partnership, or you neglect to inform your partner of an important fact. Immediately, you overapologize to your partner and then diligently put forth your best efforts to right the situation. Then, it starts—the pangs of serious guilt. STOP! STOP! STOP!

Guilt is our conscience's way of telling us of our temporarily out-of-balance emotional condition. Guilt is a good thing—to a point. Without guilt we would be soulless and callous. However, enduring guilt can be a sign of self-hate manifested as self-battering. It is as if we were saying to ourselves, "I am worthless and in desperate need of punishment. Since there is no one here who will punish me, I will take on the job myself."

There are many downsides to prolonged guilt after a mistake. Guilt robs us of the enormous energy needed for the partnership to succeed. Prolonged guilt steals our self-esteem, denying us courage, optimism, and passion. Guilt takes us to a one-down position; our partners must carry us. Picking up the emotional slack increases their anger, which, if unchecked, they eventually express, driving us to greater levels of self-doubt and guilt, and the cycle becomes a self-perpetuating, sick, interper-

"The psychological aspect of injury prevention is as important to the dancer as is proper conditioning and nutrition. Dancers, like people, have varying personalities and react to stress in unique ways."

—Daniel Arnheim, *Dance Injuries*

sonal game. Uncorrected, it can doom your partnership to a premature death.

Stumble #4: You Violate a Core Value or Protocol

Honest mistakes are one thing; a breach of a core value is another. This breed of blunder can carry a subtle message warning of much deeper issues. It is for this reason we recommend you "scrutinize" your actions and your motives for compromising a fundamental partnership agreement. Careful study of this particular pain may teach particularly important lessons.

These violations take many forms. It may be the tiny white lie born of the belief that the upset provoked by complete disclosure is a greater harm than the damage done by a minor deception. It might be the cowardly decision to remain silent rather than publicly defend a partner falsely labeled. It could be the tiny betrayal of a partner's confidence to someone who "would *never* tell a soul." It could be taking full credit when you know shared credit would be more honest.

Great partnerships are suffused with complete, total, wall-to-wall, no-exceptions integrity. Great partnerships stand on integrity, are constructed of integrity, and reek of integrity. Integrity is the color they are painted, the kind of true blue that can be seen for miles. Great partnerships do not do half-assed integrity. As Tom Peters says, "There is no such thing as a minor lapse of integrity." Partnership integrity is as uncompromising as George Washington's cherry tree.

Against this grand standard, all acts of deception, secrecy, and betrayal stand out as deeds of dishonor. They indicate one of two things: a lack of deep commitment to the partnership or a self-defeating notion that one is not good enough for a high-octane partnership. Low self-esteem can actually entice a person to set up a relationship to fail—a self-fulfilling prophecy.

If you breach of one of the six core protocols discussed in Step Three: Rehearsal—expecting excellence, honesty, respect, commitment, promises to be kept, purpose held firm—it can be a serious and dramatic indication that some other agenda is operating within. It warrants reflection, vigilance, and renewal. Breach of core protocols or values is the disease of partnership which, left unchecked, will claim its very life. Any dis-ease is your cue to stop, look, and listen.

Scrutinize and Short Circuit

How do you short circuit this breakup-waiting-to-happen malady? The "scrutinize" strategy requires thoughtful reflection and assertive energy. This might also be the time to appoint a shadow partner—a person who has no particular vested interest in either of you but a great concern for the relationship. You can use your shadow partner as a mentor to your partnership or as a sounding board for either or both of you.

Here are some other tips:

- Agree with your partner to raise concerns about a potential breach of values the minute you sense the possibility. Tell each other exactly how you hope to raise such a worry: "Jane, I might say something like 'I could be very wrong about this, but my gut tells me there's something I need to know that you are reluctant to tell me.' Is that a yellow flag you could work with?" In outlining exactly how you *hope* to reveal a concern, you gain confidence, and should you ever need to exercise the warning, you've already greased the skids with your partner.

- Err on the side of assuming that your partnership is strong enough to handle conflict. Too often, negative feelings are allowed to build up out of fear that the relationship is too fragile to weather confrontation.

- Never assume that an act of indiscretion will go unnoticed. Even if your partner completely misses your infraction, you'll waste valuable partnership energy hiding the act and feeling guilty about your inappropriate behavior. Go to your partner and lay it on the line.
- Once the air has been cleared and the issue openly discussed, go back once again and apologize. This telegraphs to your partner that you acknowledge the seriousness of the event. Learn from the incident—then move on.
- If you haven't instituted a periodic partnership checkup, this is a good time to begin one. Set aside a time to focus occasionally on the quality of your relationship.

Great dances are never flawless. Muscles ache, costumes fray, stage hands tire, and dancers sometimes just have an off night. Mature dancers manage the anguish and bounce back to dazzle again. Great partnerships are like great dances—more leather than steel, more willow than oak. Their long-term resilience rests in their capacity to bend with anguish and continue to dance even in adversity. They know that pain is more teacher than torturer—a mentor for mastery rather than an agent of agony.

Heather was a gifted dancer, but a congenital disease and years of rehearsing and performing caused crippling pain in both legs. She would actually use a wheelchair between shows. Yet, on stage, the power of the performance, the energy of the other dancers, her disciplined will and focused self-management, as well as the excitement of the audience, would enable her to push through the pain and dance. Like gymnast Kerry Strug in the 1996 Olympics, professionals will often keep going for the team while suffering great pain. But the will to prevail cannot come solely from the external support of the team or partnership. It must be joined by an internal discipline and self-generated drive.

Pain can be a friendly tutor only if you heed its early warnings, use it as a diagnostic tool, and always think of it as an important resource for partner and partnership growth. Respect pain—but never make pain your friend. Partners who welcome pain as their friend soon find it staying for supper. And when it has overstayed its welcome, pain catches you not looking and eats all the dessert!

LESSON

12 Coping with Pain That's Not Your Fault

IT IS AXIOMATIC IN DANCE THAT GREATNESS COMES ONLY through discomfort—pushing beyond the point when sinews, senses, and spirit say "stop." Pain can also have a completely different meaning. As one great dancer stated, "Aches warn us we are entering the green zone of progress. They also warn us of the entry into the red zone of permanent damage. Pros learn to read the difference, stopping for reds, pushing on beyond the greens."

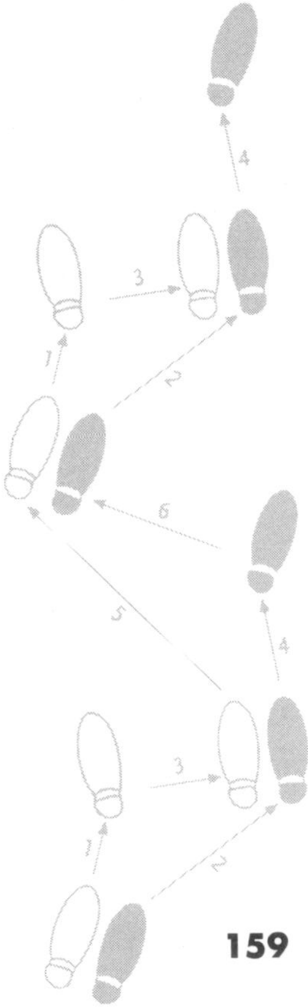

Partnership pain has similar multiple meanings. Growing pains are clearly a green light. However, red-zone pain carries destructive qualities which, if ignored, can take the partnership on the path to permanent danger. In the last lesson, we examined pain that we cause. In this lesson we will explore pain that comes at us from our partner.

When Partners Get Angry

Partnerships are sometimes the context for great anger. Partner A gets enraged and, like a loaded pistol, fires anger at Partner B, who is pained and may reciprocate. This uproar is followed by a frustrated exit, by acquiescence, by a fight, or by some other form of retaliation. The bottom line on this anger-driven pain is this: while occasionally rage is a therapeutic release, it is most typically the medium of madness, mayhem, and maybe termination. Most partnerships have disconnects from time to time that produce painful emotional irritation. The kind to watch out for is the behavior that is out of character, extreme for the circumstance, or seemingly unwarranted.

Understanding anger and how to manage it is a hallmark of great partnerships. Anger is not a primary behavior. It is a secondary behavior; the primary driver for anger is a frustrated need or motive. Anger is the way many of us express our anxiety when we—especially our most dimly lit, innermost selves—don't get what we want.

Where does anger come from? Its root is fear or anxiety. Most fears are illogical. Granted, there *are* logical fears. When you go to the dentist, your fear of discomfort and pain is logical. There are also logical "going to work" fears. People worry about getting rejected, looking foolish, losing power, appearing incompetent—a wide range of fears short of "you're going to be abused or die." Most fears, however, are not logical—they are psychological. The source of the fear is not getting an important psychological need met. Think of a priority need as a psychological default—the one you fall back on when anxiety is in the air.

The goal is to get a finer bead on your partner's priority need (drive or motive) as a path to eliminating pain (a.k.a. anger). Pay close attention to actions your partner has taken and ask: what important emotional or psychological need might be met by the action she selected? Examine the timing of moments of anger. What's going on when ire surfaces?

Keep in mind that anger is a secondary feeling; the root issue is generally a frustrated need. Achievers fear losing, affiliators fear rejection, power seekers fear appearing weak, and control freaks fear being wrong or losing dominion over their circumstances. The higher priority the need plays in your partner's life, the more fearful (and angry) she will be if she perceives that need to be threatened.

> ***"Good partnerships gone awry usually contain at least one of the following statements preceding their demise: I thought you meant, I thought you said, You told me you were going to, My contract says that, or You promised me that you would . . . ."***
>
> **—Michael Somers, Computer Curriculum Corporation**

Answering Anger

So what? Assume you now have a clearer understanding of what might drive your partner to anger. What next? Remember our earlier advice? Answer the literal words of a question while addressing a deeper issue that you think might be really fueling the fear. Assume that every statement made to the tune of anger is a song played in stereo—the obvious statement about the issue or concern at hand and the underlying response to a frustrated need. Respond to both channels in the way you communicate.

We've outlined a few thoughts on how you might make your response to anger more fruitful. We encourage you to follow our theme, but it is very important that your precise message reflect your own style and personality. Faking comments will seem contrived (which they are) and work counter to your goal of dealing effectively with partner anger.

Sashaying with a Strutter

Strutters are extremely achievement-oriented, but with a negative twist. They use anger in a competitive way, often pushing the confrontation to a right-wrong plane. If you allow the confrontation to get to that level, you will expend more energy on trying to avoid losing than on finding a collaborative, win-win solution. Surly Strutters show their egotism either by acting insolent and aloof or by ranting loudly. Let them calm down. Refuse to react to their rage and conceit. And never laugh at their juvenile antics. Their stormy mood will pass.

Bolstering a Bunny Hop and Taming a Tap Dancer

Bunny Hops are extreme affiliators with a positive twist. When they get angry, they hide it from you. They assume their anger is their own doing, so they silently seethe in private. They may want you to take the initiative to find out what's wrong—to beg it out of them. Avoid this approach. Tap Dancers are extreme affiliators with a negative twist. They express anger in more obvious ways—pouting, sulking, or grumbling in ways that are intended to make you feel guilty and responsible.

It's important with both Bunny Hops and Tap Dancers to zero in on what lies behind their smoke screens. Use some variation of this probing gambit to encourage them to open up: "I think you're more angry than you've said. It would be better for our partnership if you told me what's really wrong. When you're ready to talk about it, I'm ready to listen."

Breaking a Break Dancer

Break dancers are partners with big needs for power. They enjoy the fit of anger and the fight for domination so much that they tend to see innocent resistance as confrontation. Avoid getting into it with them except on issues involving values and ethics or any issue that has "partnership failure" written all over it. Be alert to the Break Dancer's susceptibility to see many issues as a threat to their competence, status, position, or territory.

Waltzing a Wallflower

Wallflowers are the adult version of the angry child who responds to an invitation to come along by simply sitting on the floor and refusing to budge. Their control-based anger is filled with various versions of stonewalling and stubbornly resisting. They get their partners to yield to their will by intentionally frustrating all hopes of progress. The best approach to get Wallflowers to budge is to be direct and clear about the effect their behavior is having on the partnership. Help them discover how their controlling behavior is contributing to an unpredictable, out-of-control situation.

When Partners Don't Pull Their Weight

It takes two (not one and a half) to tango! Partnerships in which one partner perceives he is carrying more than his fair share are breeding grounds for discontent and debilitating hostility.

Clearly there are times when it is acceptable for one partner to let up and let the other partner carry the load for a time. Part of the value of being in the relationship is interdependence—mutually independent and mutually dependent. Part of the partnership challenge is being very clear on what is expected of each partner. Should expectations change, partners need instant clarity to make the appropriate adjustments.

> ***"The partnership is crumbling when thoughts and conversations are about the rules of the game rather than the game itself."***
>
> **—Jay Cone, Interaction Associates**

Partnerships can never be consistently or perpetually equal. Think of partnership balance as being more like floating reciprocity. There is always a rise and fall; power shifts back and forth as the partners seek to equalize their relationship with each other. Balance is achieved through "talking during the dance." Great dancers don't count credits, they confer!

Conferring with your partner about imbalance carries special challenges. First, there is the issue of perception. One partner's 50 percent might be the other's 30 percent. Keep in mind that if your partner thinks there is imbalance, there *is* imbalance. In relationships, perception is more important than reality. Sit down with your partner and hold a diagnostic discussion. Don't start with blame, start with aim—the goal of your partnership. If you couch your feelings or perceptions within the context of what you are collectively trying to achieve, you have a much better grounding for renegotiation.

Cite examples as aids for clarity and understanding, not as proof or evidence of the rightness of your position. Work hard to keep your anger from infiltrating the conversation. It is important for your partner to know you have strong feelings about the imbalance, but your conversation will be more fruitful if you work very hard to check your animosity at the door.

Work as hard to understand your partner's point of view as you do to describe your own. Listen—and show that you're listening. Listen to learn, not to teach or make a point. Ask questions to learn more about your partner's position. Be careful to avoid any emotion-laden or inflammatory words or phrases.

If you cannot concur, chalk it up to the stars or weather and agree to revisit the subject when you both have had time to regroup and reflect. But avoid letting too much time pass. Issues like imbalance will quickly undermine a relationship if allowed to fester. If your second attempt falters, let your shadow partner play an arbitrator role with the primary goal of helping each of you hear and understand the other's position.

When Partners Get Cocky

Arrogance flipped over is insecurity, unnecessary interpersonal armor, which has many adverse outcomes on partnerships. Symbolically, it slows down the process of communication so that suspicion has time to slip in. It also trips up communication, since it forces understanding to take a rough detour to get through. Good communication is straight and pure; arrogance-based communication is obtuse and murky. When dealing with an arrogant or overconfident partner, you're never sure your meaning got through as you intended.

Since humility is required for learning, arrogance inhibits learning and growth. Arrogance radiates distrust and makes teamwork difficult. Arrogance is also associated with greed, and greed can suck the wind out of the agility needed for peak partnership performance. In a climate of greed, partners waste effort performing perpetual due diligence and constantly tracking credit. Energy is blown on issues of fairness and reciprocity.

Overcoming arrogance is possible only by pondering its origin. What is your partner defending? What would be the consequence to your partner if her self-view were projected on a movie screen? What would be the consequence if your partner replaced self-admiration with a genuine interest in others, or conceit with concern? Think of attacking your partner's arrogance with assertive warmth and joyful vulnerability. Try it on a stranger and note the reaction.

> ***"The partnership is sinking when a partner is busy managing his own return. It also is on the rocks when a partner needs to win, when he or she has to be the dominant person in the relationship. Partnership, like marriage, is not a relationship you have to win at."***
>
> **—Perry Miles, Spirit Cruises**

When Partners Stop Growing

All partnerships, at some point, struggle when one partner grows faster than the other. And unbalanced growth is second only to poor communication as the leading reason for partnership failure. Great partnerships anticipate the likelihood of unbalanced growth by continually raising the bar or changing their focus. Grady Rosier, president of McLane Company, sums up the challenge:

> We *must* keep altering our standards. The minute we stop growing and maturing is the minute we start stagnating. Since our partners are not likely to be interested in stagnating with us, we risk waking up one day to discover we are in a relationship with a stranger.

Partners never grow at exactly the same pace. But when one partner grows significantly faster than the other, while viewing the "lazy" partner as equally capable of growth, the stage is set for resentment, hostility, and ultimately conflict. When the gap reaches a certain point, it is too wide to close fast enough to save the relationship. Too many partnerships needlessly fall on their face, when early warning and redirection could have saved them.

> ***"A quick route to partnership failure is greed. When your partner says words like, 'You're making more money than I am,' your relationship is in trouble."***
>
> **—Jack Tester, Contractors 2000**

Laziness in a partnership signals several things. It can mean a partner is taking the relationship for granted. Sometimes partners find more stimulating ways to spend their energy and simply redirect their efforts. Laziness can indicate a decline in commitment—the partners' early excitement wanes as the shine wears off. Laziness can also be a response to unspoken disappointment. It is a common affliction in partnerships with Wallflowers.

No matter what the origin, laziness must be confronted. Partnership renewal is in order. If your partnership were a marriage, it might be refreshed through a second honeymoon at a resort, coupled with some straight talk about your present situation, missed opportunities, and future development. Let your partner know you're concerned about the seemingly lost sense of excitement in your relationship. Get your partner to offer his assessment of the situation. Focus on your partnership goals and the gap between the present state and the future state you both desire.

When a Core Protocol Is Breached

"A character flaw cannot be corrected," says Ed Novak of the Broker Restaurants. "If your partner is dishonest, you are looking at a character flaw. You can work through a lot of things, but not a character flaw. My advice is to seriously consider folding your tent and finding another partner." "At the core," says Mary Ann Monas of AchieveGlobal Canada, "it's all about doing the right thing for the other when the other is not around."

Can a partnership recover when a core protocol is breached? Only with great effort, we believe. While partnership generosity rests on a forgiving attitude, all partnerships lose if the victim of a protocol breach too quickly acquits and accepts. These violations are serious.

Put the issue on the table, assertively and resolutely. Let your partner experience your anger and disappointment. But don't slam the door and walk out! Strong partnerships need resilience, not abandonment. Granted, everything about the situation may be repugnant and your self-protection armor may be telling you to exit. But conflicts can't be resolved if you leave.

> ***"The character of the partnership is vital. We closely examine the character of the people we want to partner with."***
>
> **—Terry McElroy, McLane Company**

Give your partner the benefit of the doubt. Don't assume that your initial assessment is completely accurate. There may truly be extenuating circumstances that might shed a completely different light on the infraction. Hear your partner out—and work to keep your anger and pain from seducing you into hearing what you want to hear.

This is not intended to encourage gullibility. Openness is the door to understanding, not the doormat welcoming naive blindness. Be strong enough to hear—*and* be strong enough to hold firm to the values and agreements you established at the beginning of the partnership. When you hear your partner make excuses, point to the agreements you made. When you hear your partner rationalize, point to your agreements again. Focus on the impact the infraction has had on your partnership, not just on you personally. If you expect the dance to resume, refrains like "poor me" will not be the music likely to get the two of you on the floor again.

Be patient while your partner recovers. Getting up from such a fall from grace is not likely to happen without some wobbling and wavering. But do not, even for one second, lower your standards. The partnership will ultimately gain from your strength as you carry both of you for a while.

Finally, accept the fact that the partnership may have been damaged beyond repair. Some infractions can be so severe that the very best attempts at recovery may not be adequate. As Frank Esposito, president of Tucker Rocky Distributing, says, "No matter how good the person or partnership was, some damage may just be irreparable."

"If the partnership needs to end, kill it," advises consultant Geoff Bellman. "Don't let it die on its own." There are other dances to be danced. Leave the floor with your dignity and self-respect intact. Make clear to your partner the reason for your premature exit. As Melinda Goddard of Roche Laboratories suggests, "It is important partners are as honest about ending the relationship as we are about starting it. Otherwise, they can be 'suspended' and never really end."

Find a time when you can reflect on the partnership to derive lessons that can be important in your next partnership. Armed with twenty-twenty hindsight, pay particular attention to recalling the audition. Was there anything your partner said or didn't say, did or didn't do, that could have provided an early warning? Examine your motives for having sought a partnership in the first place. What can you do differently in the future to avoid getting into a partnership that has the makings of an unnecessarily painful ending? Finally, look on this experience as an important learning opportunity. Let it go and move on.

Dancers know that hurting is a natural nuisance that comes with greatness. Only by pushing beyond your comfort zone can excellence spring forth. And sooner or later even the best dance partner steps on your foot. Pain is also a customary component of partnerships that refuse to be satisfied with second-rate or so-so performance.

Wise partnerships do not avoid pain; they learn to manage pain effectively. They avoid practices that lead to relationship-destroying injury and choose instead the instructive pain of partnership-stretching ones. Learning from their discomfort, they do not seek to suffer; they seek to excel.

The Highroad of Hurting

Great partnerships value pain, not injury. When there's pain, choose learning or leaving. There are no other healthy moves.

The lessons of partnership pain begin immediately following guilt . . . get over it!

The lessons of partnership pain begin immediately following anger . . . get past it!

All the important instructions for partnership pain management are contained in the core protocols . . . live them.

Keep forgiveness in your partnership . . . beginning with yourself.

STEP Six

DANCE LESSONS

"A painting can be finished, but a dance can never be finished at rehearsal. Dance is a creation that needs the audience to be there, and only then can there be the whole creation."

—Kei Takei

BOWING OUT

Calling It Curtains

It was a perfect close to a perfect evening at the end of a long season. The two had danced their hearts out this final performance, and the audience rewarded them with thunderous applause that seemed as if it would never end. Time after time they returned for another curtain call. The stage was beginning to look more red than tan as roses thrown from the audience piled up on the wood floor.

How had this magic happened? It seemed only yesterday the pair had scrambled to be seated next to each other at tryouts. They spoke of their histories and their hopes. But mostly they talked of their borderline hysteria over the trial of tryout. Now, they made their way to their respective dressing rooms

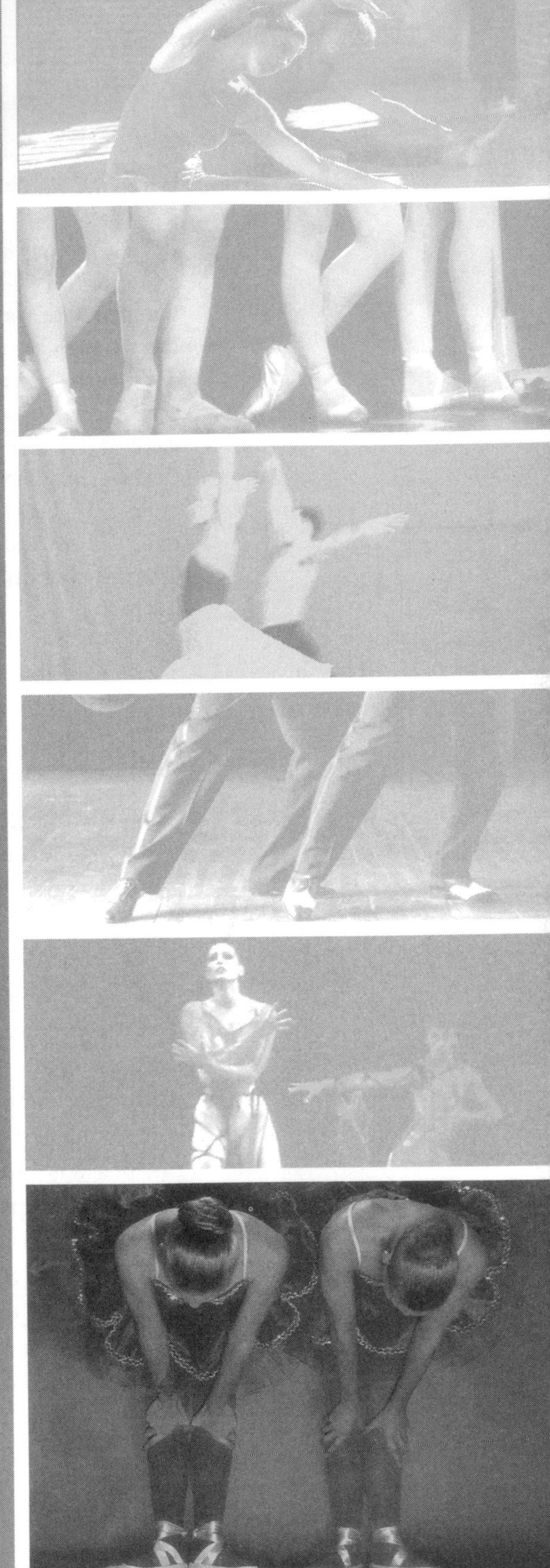

in a hurried blend of triumph, sweat, and relief.

"You gave my heart new beats," he said to her poetically as they paused in the dimly lit hallway. "You helped me find the magic again," she replied with a similar tone of melancholy. They embraced in a moment far more poignant than their calculated embraces on stage. Her "Be well" was uttered at the exact same moment as his "Take care." The end of their partnership had been choreographed as carefully as it had begun.

Great partnerships don't just stop; they end as purposefully and deliberately as they began. Their closure is planned and orchestrated to ensure there are no loose ends, no unfinished business, no unresolved problems. The bowing out phase is carefully crafted to ensure the partnership is nurtured until it is no more.

The word "nurture" implies a key concept in dancing and in partnership: relationships must be fed and cared for. Absent support and growth, partnerships languish and cease. Partnerships generally do not end in conflict; they vanilla to death. They end far more often because of neglect than strife, so the most important lesson is to keep partnerships healthy along the way.

But even healthy partnerships must sometimes be dissolved. William Shakespeare's oft-quoted line "parting is such sweet sorrow" reminds us that ending a successful partnership can be as emotionally challenging as losing a mate through death or divorce.

Bowing out on a partnership that failed can be equally difficult, because the partners may feel relief or antipathy coloring their sense of failure. Because partnerships are rich, engaging, and intimate, ending even the briefest one is not without emotion.

In these final two lessons we will explore some ways to manage partnership adjournment effectively. Lesson 13 will cover ideas for ending partnerships that failed; the final lesson will outline ways to keep the "good" in "goodbye" when closing out a successful partnership.

Exiting a partnership and ending one have the same outcome: we get out. But even though the two processes are different, they can both be managed to benefit future partnering if you approach the finale with a focus on finding the lessons to be learned.

LESSON

13 Ending a Partnership That Flopped

IT HAD THE EARLY LOOK OF SUCCESS: A FAST-GROWING PUBlishing company with a unique niche, poised for partnership with two well-known authors (one of this book's authors) to create a brand-new training program—low cost, high quality, easy to use. The company had so far published only textbooks and workbooks. This was to be their first attempt to apply the book distribution model to a packaged training program.

Their contract negotiation was seamless. An advance was arranged, program specs clarified, and one of the authors' clients chosen to field test the six-module program. Program development went smoothly; the product emerged competitively priced and attractively packaged. Everyone was proud of the new "baby"!

But as the marketing phase began, so too did the partnership death knell. The first sound

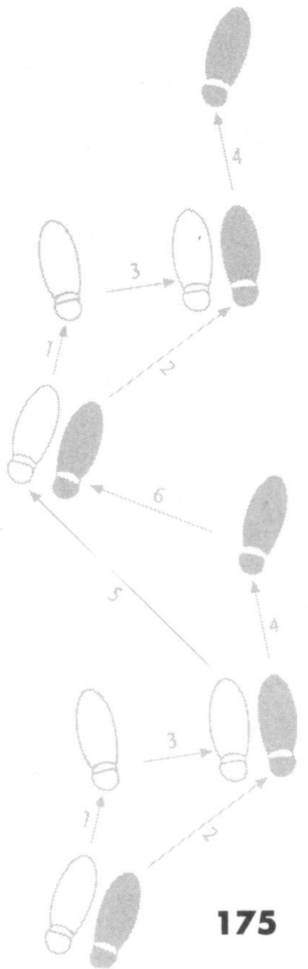

of impending failure was when the publisher asked for the authors' mailing lists. The request was not unusual; the desperation in the publisher's voice was. Because initial sales were sluggish, the publisher's communication became more terse; the authors' disappointment became more audible.

Finally, communication between publisher and authors all but ceased. As the product went into the "slow inventory" warehouse, everyone involved felt part of the partnership failure. The company's financial loss was equal to the authors' waste of sweat equity. No one was happy with the outcome.

At a trainers' conference several months later, one of the authors encountered a key executive from the publishing company. Their awkward rendezvous soon turned into a curiosity-driven debriefing. What went wrong? How did they miscue? What were the real reasons a partnership with such promise ended with such disappointment? The postmortem diagnosis soon became clear.

The publisher had assumed that the two authors would carry the lion's share of the marketing function, just as they had done for product development. "After all," said the publishing exec in defense of his perspective, "you two have such great contacts . . . and you're well known in this specialty." When author-driven marketing failed to materialize, the publisher felt betrayed by the authors. The authors were involved in several other business partnerships and had assumed that once the product hit the market, their marketing role would be more passive than active—more support than leadership. They felt abandoned by the publisher.

"If we had communicated up front the way we're communicating now," said the publishing executive, "we would not be communicating now about what we're communicating!" Both agreed that each had ignored early signals that could have forewarned an impending stumble. Both agreed that they had not been forthright about the concerns they were feeling. The publishing executive summed it up this way: "This partnership could have worked. It's a shame our expectations discussion only covered our aspirations, not our assumptions. We were both too timid for our own good."

Our research on partnership revealed a special discovery: endings can be as important as beginnings. Partnerships sometimes deteriorate to animosity because the partners are unable to recognize ending signals and dance on after the music has stopped. The ill-starred stoppage leaves the partners angry, bitter, and reluctant to dance again. Sometimes partnerships just peter out without anyone drawing the curtains. Adjournments are as vital as auditions—whether closure comes because of failure or in spite of success.

Handling the Dark Side of Closure

"When your partnership fails, take a close look at your own footprints," suggests Jack Tester of Contractors 2000. "If you think it is over, look at your motives, look at theirs, trust your gut, and pull the trigger." His advice to extract personal growth from a partnership failure is wise counsel.

The key to avoiding the bitter side of ending a failing partnership is recognizing the signs of needed closure. There are at least three forces that can precipitate this "sweet sorrow":

- Partner A wants the partnership to end, but Partner B does not (or the reverse);
- neither partner wants to end, but external forces demand it; or
- both partners want the partnership to end because they recognize that it has failed and external forces share their view.

Understanding the impetus for closure can help you shape the proper parting, and there are special considerations for bowing out of each scene.

Partner A Wants to End, Partner B Does Not

This scenario can be the most awkward in partnership closings. Reminiscent of the desolate timbre of unrequited love, disagreements over endings can fuel possessiveness, blaming, and ultimately animosity. Victims of the slamming door of an impending partnership divorce typically have been getting exit signs for some time. Unfortunately, denial and disbelief have deafened them to the dissonant chords. Fearing the truth, they either fail to periodically assess the relationship, or they opt for timidity over assertive and continuous candor.

If there were ever a case for doing a periodic partnership checkup, this is it! No one likes to be the one left behind. A periodic partnership review can reveal early signs of discord and set the stage for partnership renewal. If the cancer of discontent progresses too far, no amount of renewal surgery can turn the condition around.

How does a partner cue a colleague during this precarious step? If you're the one who wants the partnership to continue, your best tactic in deferring the departure of a partner hellbent on leaving is to fervently restate your commitment to the partnership and then focus on the rational benefits of continuing. Any show of sentiment, any hint of guilt or blame, is likely to snuff the partnership candle entirely. It is valuable for your partner to know your deep commitment. However, the most effective way to slow your partner's exit is through reasonable logic. If a sensible approach fails to make sense, move your energy into choreographing a healthy ending. You will both gain if you can help the relationship to a comfortable finale, not an abrupt stop.

What does all this sound like? Listen as two partners discuss leaving, each from a different motivation and desire to continue.

Partner B: *"I believe we have a lot left to do together, and I'm committed to getting through this temporary hump in the road and moving forward."*

Partner A: *"I think it's over! We just need to go our separate ways now."*

Partner B: *"Let's give it a chance to work. This partnership is important to me, and I'm going to fight hard to save it. Besides, we're close to consummating the New South deal, and it's a great challenge to do something unique and powerful."*

If you are Partner A, shame on you! (We did not want you to escape without at least a tiny guilt trip—we're usually for the underdog! And we just advised the partner you want to leave behind to steer clear of such emotion.) All kidding aside, you have an important leadership role to perform on behalf of the partnership. Partnership disappointment, especially of this type, can fuel partnership dependence. Your partner may demonstrate surprising weakness, wrath, and withdrawal. These are normal reactions. If you play into your partner's emotions, however, you will simply delay the inevitable with even greater negative emotion.

What does this sound like? Listen to A and B discussing bowing out.

Partner B: *"How can it end like this? We pledged to go the distance. Remember the 'through thick and thin' part?"*

Partner A: *"I care about your feelings. And I can appreciate how tough this is. We've been through a lot, and I value what we achieved together."*

Partner B: *"But it doesn't have to end here! We can do much more together. You're leaving me in the lurch!"*

"A partnership deteriorates when you stop talking. Always reiterate why you went into the partnership. If it is not working, shake hands, respect each other, and stay friends—or, at least, not enemies. Try not to alienate your partner. Who knows, you may end up partnering again."

— John King,
J.Kings Foodservice Professionals

Partner A: *"I'm sorry you feel that way. I'm in a different place. I believe the partnership has achieved all it can, and we need to go our separate ways. We'll both benefit by closing this chapter now rather than later, when we risk separating as enemies."*

Notice that the focus of Partner A is more on the partnership than on the partner. It's important to show strength, not just sentiment. Partner A demonstrated empathy and concern without acquiescing to sympathy (shared pain). When you are the one who wants to end the partnership, it's important that you show the same sensitivity you demonstrated early in the relationship, when you were focused on looking forward.

"Be true to your mission and values all the way to the end. When you have had a parting of the ways, facilitate the discussion around mission and values. Agree to disagree relative to the mission."

— Ray Huizenga, National Granger Insurance

The Bitter End

Ending a negative partnership, or one in which negative ending feelings are inevitable, can be more difficult. Discuss it face to face; don't hide behind lawyers or communicate through letters and email. If the partnership's ending provokes anger in your partner, allow him adequate time to cool off.

Michael Somers of Computer Curriculum Corporation is a fan of candor in these situations: "If the partnership is ending because of a breakdown, be very, very specific. Do not leave your partner wondering why. Clarity in communications is important in all stages of the partnership, but it is particularly important at the end."

Carefully review the agreements outlined in your Audition and Rehearsal stages. They should have language specifying the "what ifs" of a partnership breakup, including how the partnership assets would be valued and divided. If your partnership agreement fails to speak to issues that are now points of contention, seek the counsel of an attorney. Your shadow partner could be a key resource to help iron out thorny disagreements. Or you might want to get the help of a professional mediator.

What if your ex-partner is poisoning some of your important relationships? Keep your professional integrity and resist the temptation to disparage your partner. As Covance corporate VP and general manager Carlo Medici puts it: "Avoid negative WORK of mouth!" Anticipate partner vindictiveness and give your customers, colleagues, and clients early warning. And be brief in telling your side of the story. You gain nothing (and potentially lose a lot) by attacking your partner when you're briefing others on your situation.

Both Want Out, or Outside Forces Demand It

In this ending scenario, both partners may want the partnership to end. They recognize that it has failed and external forces share their view.

This can be a tricky situation. The partners' first reaction may be: "This is a simple situation of oil and water. It didn't work. Let's just call it quits and be done with it." Not so fast—such a simplistic, task-oriented approach may have grave consequences down the road. A failed partnership—even when both partners agree it is a failure—can leave residual negative feelings that can rob you of the possibility of reconnecting as well as create undue cynicism about future partnerships with others.

What Went Wrong That Could Have Gone Right?

On the flip side, a failed partnership can be a great stage for learning. As challenging as it may seem, insight can emerge from a focused debriefing. Even if the reasons for exit seem obvious now, the underlying reasons may not be. What you learn may provide useful early warnings for your next partnership.

Use the questions below to guide your exit interview. Our recommendation is that you complete the statements separately and then get together to explore your answers.

If I had this partnership to do over again, I would have

- asked you to tell me more about . . .
- told you more about . . .
- spoken up more forcefully when . . .
- involved others in a way that . . .
- changed the way I . . .
- trusted my gut when it told me to . . .
- researched more about . . .

As I reflect on this partnership,

- what I learned about myself that I did not know (or knew, but forgot) is . . .
- what most surprised me about our partnership was . . .
- I realize I failed to . . .
- I realize the one thing I did too much was . . .
- I realize we needed an agreement which . . .
- I see we could have benefited from help when . . .
- we could have called it quits earlier if we had . . .

Can a failing partnership ever gain from going forward? Sometimes. Ask yourself: "Suppose we get past this bump, will this path take our partnership to a profitable place we might have missed if we exited now?" Put your feelings about your partner in the back seat for a moment and while firmly gripping the steering wheel examine where this route is taking you.

LESSON

Ending a Partnership That Worked 14

THE SUN WAS BEGINNING TO SET ON THE SKYLINE OUTSIDE the window of the restaurant atop a midtown office complex. Cary and Dale had just sat down to toast the closing of their success. Each had driven from their respective offices in different parts of the city.

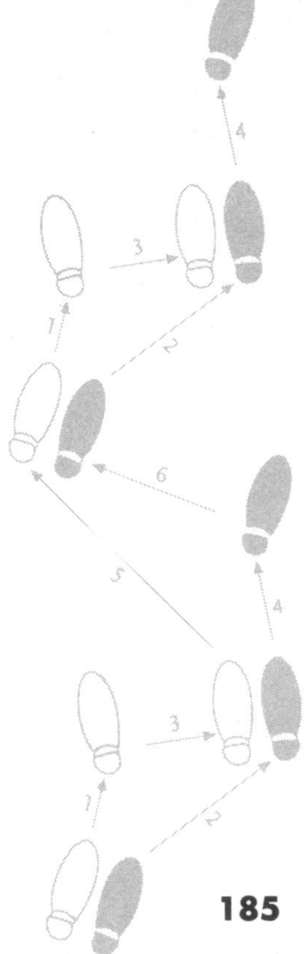

Dale: *"Great to see you. How's the Rainey project coming along? You were a bit concerned the last time we talked."*

Cary: *"Thanks for asking. It's turned out to be a major success for our company—and an incredible coup, I might add! It's opened several very promising markets for us."*

Dale: *"That's fantastic! I know you worked hard on making that one happen!"*

Cary: *"I sure did. But we would never have gotten that deal without all the stuff we were learning from your people! We owe a lot of our success to you."*

Dale: *"Thanks—but pay your homage to our partnership, not to my company! It's the partnership that made it happen. To the partnership!" (They both raise their glasses in a toast.)*

Cary: *"You're kind, Dale! And . . . it really has worked, hasn't it?"*

Dale: *"You bet! Remember when we first met and you kept me waiting for twenty minutes? I must admit I had my doubts!"*

Cary: *"Yeah, and remember in our second meeting when you accused me of being a wimp with my attorney?"*

Dale: *"Well, you were, Cary! You were!"*

Cary: *"I guess I was. But I've gotten meaner . . . with your help!"*

Dale: *"Meaner was not my intent—just tougher! And you've come a long way. But since we're on a candid note, I'd like your feedback on what I could have done to be a better partner. We promised when we started, we'd make feedback a priority, and . . ."*

> ***"Ending a partnership should be the same as it began if it has been successful . . . same goals and same purpose."***
>
> —Bob Ellis, *Daily American*

Ending a successful partnership can be a jubilant adjournment, filled with nostalgia, celebration, and affirmation. The positive side of bowing out is reflected in our last look at Dale and Cary before they go their separate ways. The partnership has achieved what was needed, and it's time to move on.

However, closure that focuses only on the saccharine side of "sweet sorrow" misses the opportunity of maximizing the "many happy returns." The grand finale of any successful alliance should be grandly filled with the wisdom of constructive critique, not just the wine of toasts. As difficult and demanding as ending a failed partnership may seem, ending a successful one can require even greater courage and discipline. Smart partners draw from the equity of their good will to use a friendly exit as an occasion to *educate*, *evaluate*, *anticipate*, and *celebrate!*

The Complete Adjournment

FOCUS	Educate	Evaluate	Anticipate	Celebrate
TO DETERMINE . . .	What's missing	What's broken	What's possible	What's great
BY-PRODUCT	Instruct	Improve	Invent	Inspire
TOOLS	Adding	Assessing	Altering	Affirming

Ending and Educating

A great partnership is a perpetually learning partnership. Even as they begin closing the curtains, dismantling the set, and hanging up the dance shoes, great partners are still educating themselves. They use adjournment as a time to examine what was missing from the relationship; they want to know what they could have added to their partnership that could have made it even better.

To be instructive, endings have to be constructed so there is time to ask, "What can we learn from this?" There are many ways to do this. It can be as simple as seeking out another successful partnership and asking them to join you in brainstorming ways you and your partner could have worked together better. One partnership treated themselves to a week-end workshop on partnering, which provided a setting to talk about lessons learned as well as a forum for them to begin to disengage.

What If . . .

Endings are also an opportunity to explore potential. Review the list below independently. Select the ones that hit a nerve as you read them. Then meet with your partner and talk about the ones you both found intriguing. These questions are aimed at surfacing the "what's missing" components of a partnership's "continuing education."

What *could* we have learned if we had . . .

- taken more risks?
- involved more people? involved fewer people?
- had a partnership checkup midway through our relationship?
- been more candid?
- learned together? not been so "together" focused?
- tried harder? not tried so hard?
- taken things slower? gone a little faster?
- taken the partnership in stages?
- shown more trust?
- been more public with others? been more private?
- had clearer criteria for partnership success?
- used better measures? not worried about measures?
- set standards around values instead of performance?

- put our agreements in writing? worked from a simple handshake?
- worked more interdependently? worked more independently?

Great partnership endings should be reflective. Too often partners rush to disengage as they approach the end. Remember the last time you left an organization? Even though you may have had a nice goodbye party, people had probably already started distancing themselves, as if you had already left. This behavior is a normal way of coping with separation; we prematurely acclimate ourselves to the departure of another. But this natural coping mechanism can cause us to rush to adjournment, missing out on useful insights. Force yourself to remember, reflect, and review.

Ending and Evaluating

Every partnership has components in need of correction. If not, the partnership is surely dancing a timid, mechanical dance; it has no heart! Blemish-free partnerships are focusing on the accuracy of their footwork, not the spirit of their dance. Great partnerships are *very* human . . . meaning they are genuine, and thus blemished; real, therefore unfinished. Endings are a chance to evaluate what *was* so you can discover what should have been.

As you conduct your evaluation, it is important to remember that your final partnership critique is an effort aimed at improvement, not an exercise in condemnation. Assess to find gaps, not guilt; appraise to uncover blemishes, not blame. While judgment is in fact the goal, it should not be the tone. Focus on analyzing the partnership, not the partners. Endings that allow partner to judge partner can quickly deteriorate into a rebuke-and-reprisal session—not a healthy way to say farewell. However, if you focus your parting critique on improving the relationship, there are valuable lessons to be learned. Go back to your partnership test (lessons 4 and 5) and revisit those questions as a tool for evaluating your partnership.

Ending and Anticipating

A third part of great partnership adjournment is to focus on what might have been possible. This form of anticipation can be an inventive way to propel the partners to enter future partnerships with new insights and innovative approaches. Great partners take time to dream about what the partnership might have been. Such dreaming can be a boon to forming creative partnerships and innovative alliances in the future.

More What Ifs . . .

Attribute listing, an old creativity technique, can provide a way to alter the way we think about our partners and unleash new, more inventive approaches. Force-fitting selected attributes to the partnership gives rise to new applications.

Below is a list of attributes to be used as triggers for innovative partnership ideas. Use the list to force each trigger word or phrase to apply to your partnership. Even if your first thought is "Naw, that's not relevant," go ahead and try to think about what your partnership could be like if you forced the attribute to fit. You may be surprised at what you discover.

What if we had partnered in a manner so that our partnership was . . .

Faster	More fun	Divided into parts
Slower	More inspirational	Done with a guide

Quicker	More instructional	Done with a manual
Longer	More inclusive	Done anywhere/remotely
Smaller	More invisible	Done with something else
Larger	More elegant/classy	Done automatically
Cheaper	More responsive	Completely tailored
Bolder	More attractive	Done backwards
Funnier	More efficient	Done while you wait

Great partners also ensure the partnership closes with linkages to other resources and relationships. As they ride off into their respective sunsets, great partners demonstrate concern for the quality of what's on their partner's horizon. They are quick to offer support beyond their relationship. "You might want to call Joe . . . ," "I'll send an update on . . . ," or "Next time you're in Chicago . . ." flavor their closing conversations.

One mark of a great partnership is partners agreeing at the end of an assignment, project, or effort to pursue a possible return engagement. In the words of Melissa Moss, president of the Women's Consumer Network, "It's very special when your partner says, 'Well, we just completed that, but I have a great idea about how we can work together on another thing' and they take the initiative to get it started." When partners agree to stay on the dance floor for the next song, you have a relationship you can cherish, nourish, and celebrate.

"If your partnership is built on trust, endings will not be a surprise nor close with bad feelings. Effective endings are based on mutual agreement that each has fulfilled the other's needs."

—Dennis Bolling, Producers Livestock Association

Ending and Applause

"Take time to celebrate what has been great together," advises Atlanta Community Food Bank's Bill Bolling. Celebrate with fanfare and stories.

Celebration need not be a party with band and banner. Celebration can be as simple as dinner at a special restaurant, a drink after work, a picnic lunch in a nearby park. The point of celebration is that it be clearly an event associated with the conclusion of the partnership. This rite of passage is a powerful symbol in gaining closure and moving on to the next plateau. Celebration should include compliments, stories, and food. Weave the celebration with laughter and joy.

> ***"Perform to the end. Create a spectacular departure. Congratulate each other on what went well. Acknowledge what went wrong and depart with respect."***
>
> **—Jack Dowling, CompuCom**

Lace your final meeting or two with opportunities to remember, reflect, and refocus. Let your recall questions bridge the discussion toward the future. Zeroing in solely on the past can mire your parting in melancholy. Just as early rapport was crucial to a successful beginning of a partnership, an upbeat adjournment is equally important for the ending. Letting go is rarely comfortable, but it's always important to enable your partner to flourish and continue to grow out of the shadow of your partnership. Mark the moment by managing adjournment as a visible expression of goal achievement and happiness.

William James, the great philosopher-psychologist, said, "The deepest craving of human nature is the need to be appreciated." Celebrating the end of your partnership run is not the time to assume "my partner knows she is valued." It is about actions. Celebration begins with "see"—actions that telegraph to partners they are important. Bow to your partner and acknowledge his or her contribution. Bow to your partnership in gratitude for its distinctive gift to you both!

The Bedrocks of Bowing Out

Great partnerships don't just stop . . . they end purposefully and gracefully.

Ending a partnership that failed requires great courage. Ending a partnership that succeeded takes even more.

When the curtains are closing, great dancers bow to their audience; great partners bow to each other.

Celebration begins with "see" . . . observable action is better than assumed admiration.

Partnerships, like dances, are lessons of the heart. And the heart is never finished learning.

Promenade Home

In a ragtime style

Words by Heather Shea
Music by Chip R. Bell

F G C7 F G
It's fi-nished, last en - core let's prom - e - nade home! We did it, great team-work
Piano
mf
C7 F C A Dm G7
the best we have known. We learned a lot a-bout how sy-ner-gy can pay, We're sure our
C C7 F G C7 F
next al - li - ance takes a smooth-er way It's fi-nished, last en-core let's prom-e-nade home!
cresc.
mf

NOTES

Page

10 Legally, a partnership: Bromberg, *Crane and Bromberg on Partnership*, 1.

11 Scheuing defines a "joint venture": *Power of Strategic Partnering*, 17.

87 When Ken Blanchard characterized feedback: Blanchard and Johnson, *One Minute Manager*, 44.

105 Keeping agreements . . . is joining forces: Hendricks and Ludeman, *Corporate Mystic*, 45.

122 The success of an alliance: Lewis, *Partnerships for Profit*, 108.

131 Love is long suffering and kind: Jordan, *Cotton Patch Version*, 66.

133 Until one is committed: Murray, *Scottish Himalayan Expedition*, 312.

SOURCES

Interviews

Jane Anderson, senior vice president, Saint Vincent Health System, Erie, Penn.

Eunice Azzani, vice president/partner, Korn/Ferry International, San Francisco, Calif.

Ellyn Bader, The Couples Institute, Menlo Park, Calif.

Geoffrey M. Bellman, author and consultant, Seattle, Wash.

Marjorie Blanchard, chairman of the board, Blanchard Training and Development, Escondido, Calif.

Bill Bolling, executive director, Atlanta Community Food Bank, Atlanta, Ga.

Dennis Bolling, chief executive officer, Producers Livestock Association, Columbus, Ohio

Diana Boyce, executive director, Corporate Alliances for Celebration Health, Orlando, Fla.

Chris Calabrese, general manager, Marriott CasaMagna, Puerto Vallarta, Mexico

John Campbell, president, Brookfield Management Services, Toronto, Canada

Tony Codianni, director, training and dealer development group, Toshiba Information Systems, Inc., Irvine, Calif.

Javier Cano, general manager, Marina Beach Marriott Hotel, Marina del Rey, Calif.

Gene Columbus, manager of entertainment staffing, Walt Disney World Entertainment, Lake Buena Vista, Fla.

Jay Cone, senior associate, Interaction Associates, Dallas, Tex.

Marcia Corbett, vice president for marketing, AchieveGlobal, Tampa, Fla.

Steve Curtin, training manager, Marriott International, New York, N.Y.

Tony D'Amelio, vice president, Washington Speakers Bureau, Alexandria, Va.

Sharon A. Decker, president, The Lynnwood Foundation, Charlotte, N.C.

Jack Dowling, chief information officer, CompuCom, Dallas, Tex.

Bob Ellis, managing editor, *The Daily American*, West Frankfort, Ill.

Frank Esposito, president and chief operating officer, Tucker Rocky Distributing, Fort Worth, Tex.

Kevin Freiberg, president, San Diego Consulting Group, San Diego, Calif.

Jerry Fritzler, manager, Broker Restaurants, Denver, Col.

Melinda K. M. Goddard, director, service quality and customer satisfaction, Roche Laboratories, Inc., Nutley, N.J.

Pat Heim, president, The Heim Group, Pacific Palisades, Calif.

Bunny (Patricia) Holman, co-chairman, WYNCOM, Inc., Lexington, Ky.

Ray Huizenga, director of human resources, National Granger Insurance Company, Keene, N.H.

Syd L. Kershaw, vice president, Parker Hannifin Corporation, Cleveland, Ohio

John King, president, J.Kings Foodservice Professionals, Inc., Holtzville, N.Y.

Louise Lague, president, The Wisdom Group, Old Greenwich, Conn.

Sherry McCool, general manager, Marriott Pavilion Hotel, St. Louis, Mo.

Terry McElroy, senior vice president for grocery operations, McLane Company, Inc., Temple, Tex.

Carlo Medici, corporate vice president and general manager, Covance, Princeton, N.J.

J. Michael Metzler, president, Metzler & Company, Toronto, Canada

Perry Miles, president, Spirit Cruises, Norfolk, Va.

Dee Miller, director, leadership and human skills development, USAA, San Antonio, Tex.

Mary Ann Monas, senior consultant, AchieveGlobal, Agincourt, Ont., Canada

Melissa Moss, president, Women's Consumer Network, Washington, D.C.

Ed Novak, chief executive officer, Broker Restaurants, Denver, Col.

Hank Payne, program manager, Federal Aviation Administration, Oklahoma City, Okla.

Terry Pearce, president, Leadership Communication, San Francisco, Calif.

Boyd A. Pollard, treasurer and chief financial officer, Power & Telephone Supply, Memphis, Tenn.

Lillian Prymak, vice president, Executive Forum, Englewood, Col.

Bob Reed, manager of new business development, Walt Disney World, Lake Buena Vista, Fla.

Grady Rosier, president and chief executive officer, McLane Company, Inc., Temple, Tex.

Steven J. Sherwood, president, CWS Communities Trust, Newport Beach, Calif.

Robbie Smith, senior training program specialist, U.S. Department of Energy, Albuquerque, N.M.

Michael Somers, vice president of technical operations, Computer Curriculum Corporation, Sunnyvale, Calif.

Bill Tate, chairman and CEO, Convention Planning Services, Orlando, Fla.

Jack Tester, executive director, Contractors 2000, St. Paul, Minn.

Kris Thompson, manager, Broker Restaurants, Denver, Col.

Ted Townsend, president, Townsend Engineering Company, Des Moines, Iowa

Other Sources

Arnheim, Daniel D. *Dance Injuries: Their Prevention and Cure.* 3rd ed. Pennington, N.J.: Princeton Book Co., 1991.

Bell, Chip R. *Customers As Partners: Building Relationships That Last.* San Francisco: Berrett-Koehler, 1994.

Bell, Chip R. *Managers As Mentors: Building Partnerships for Learning.* San Francisco: Berrett-Koehler, 1996.

Bellman, Geoffrey M. *Your Signature Path: Gaining New Perspectives on Life and Work.* San Francisco: Berrett-Koehler, 1996.

Bergquist, William, Juli Betwee, and David Meuel. *Building Strategic Relationships.* San Francisco: Jossey-Bass, 1995.

Black, Henry L., Henry Campbell Black, and Jacqueline M. Nolan-Haley. *Black's Law Dictionary.* 6th ed. Belmont, Calif.: West/ Wadsworth, 1991.

Blanchard, Kenneth, and Spencer Johnson. *The One Minute Manager.* New York: Berkley Books, 1981.

Borrows, F. *History of Ballroom Dancing: The Dancing Master.* New York: Gordon Press, 1986.

Bromberg, Alan R. *Crane and Bromberg on Partnership.* St. Paul, Minn.: West Publishing Co., 1968.

The Dance Notebook. Philadelphia: Running Press, 1984.

Facciuto, Eugene "Luigi," Lorraine Person Kriegel, and Francis James Roach. *Luigi's Jazz Warm Up: An Introduction to Jazz Style and Technique.* Pennington, N.J.: Princeton Book Co., 1997.

Freiberg, Kevin, and Jackie Freiberg. *Nuts! Southwest Airlines' Crazy Recipe for Business and Personal Success.* Austin, Tex.: Bard Press, 1996.

Giordano, Gus. *Jazz Dance Class: Beginning through Advanced.* Pennington, N.J.: Princeton Book Co., 1992.

Grody, Svetlana McLee, Dorothy Daniels Lister, and Frank Rich. *Conversations with Choreographers.* Portsmouth, N.H.: Heinemann, 1996.

Harari, Oren. *Leapfrogging the Competition: Five Giant Steps to Market Leadership.* Washington, D.C.: American Century Press, 1997.

Heim, Patricia, and Susan K. Galant. *Hardball for Women: Winning at the Game of Business*. New York: Plume, 1993.

Hendricks, Gay, and Kate Ludeman. *The Corporate Mystic*. New York: Bantam, 1996.

Jonas, Gerald. *Dancing: The Pleasure, Power, and Art of Movement*. New York: Smithmark, 1997

Jordan, Clarence. *The Cotton Patch Version of the New Testament*. Americus, Ga.: Koinonia Partners, 1969.

Lewis, Jordan. *Partnerships for Profit*. New York: Free Press, 1990.

Moody, Patricia E. *Breakthrough Partnering*. Essex Junction, Vt.: Omneo, 1993.

Murray, W. H. *The Scottish Himalayan Expedition*. London: MacMillan & Sons., 1950.

Pearce, Terry. *Leading Out Loud: The Authentic Speaker, the Credible Leader*. San Francisco: Jossey-Bass, 1995.

Rackham, Neal, Lawrence Freidman, and Richard Ruff. *Getting Partnering Right*. New York: McGraw-Hill, 1996.

Scheuing, Eberhard E. *The Power of Strategic Partnering*. Portland, Ore.: Productivity Press, 1994.

Schultze, Horst. Presentation at the annual conference of the American Society for Training and Development, Orlando, Fla., May 1990.

Stoltz, Paul, and David Pulatie. *Adversity Quotient: Turning Obstacles into Opportunities*. New York: Wiley, 1997.

Taylor, Jim, and Ceci Taylor. *Psychology of Dance*. Champaign, Ill.: Human Kinetics, 1995.

Wilson, Larry, and Hersch Wilson. *Stop Selling, Start Partnering*. Essex Junction, Vt.: Omneo, 1994.

Zemke, Ron, and Kristin Anderson. *Coaching Knock Your Socks Off Service*. New York: AMACOM, 1997.

AUTHORS

Chip R. Bell is a senior partner with Performance Research Associates and manages their Dallas, Texas, office. Prior to starting a consulting firm in the late 1970s, he was vice president and director of management and organization development for NCNB Corporation (now NationsBank). He is the author or co-author of eleven books, including three best-sellers: *Managers As Mentors*, *Customers As Partners*, and (with Ron Zemke) *Managing Knock Your Socks Off Service*. He has served as a consultant or trainer to many Fortune 100 companies, including IBM, Cadillac, Microsoft, Motorola, Sprint, Lucent Technologies, USAA, Harley-Davidson, Marriott, 3M, Eli Lily, Price Waterhouse, Ritz-Carlton Hotels, and Victoria's Secret.

Heather Shea is CEO of Inspiritrix, Inc., an Orlando, Florida–based management training, development, and consulting firm. She is the former president of The Tom Peters Group training and consulting company and has also held senior-level positions with Arthur Andersen, CIGNA, and First National Bank of Chicago. A former professional dancer and actress, she is a world-class speaker and has delivered seminars and keynote speeches to such clients as 3M, Bank of America, Ford, Toshiba, MTV, Chevron, AIG, and Walt Disney World.

INDEX

To contact the authors . . .

Chip R. Bell

Performance Research Associates, Inc.
25 Highland Park #100
Dallas, TX 75205-2785

Phone: (214) 522-5777
Fax: (214) 691-7591
Email: PRAWest@aol.com

Heather Shea

Inspiritrix, Inc.
7512 Dr. Phillips Blvd. #129
Orlando, FL 32819

Phone: (407) 363-7141
Fax: (407) 363-0256
Email: Shea8846@aol.com

Berrett-Koehler Publishers

Berrett-Koehler is an independent publisher of books, periodicals, and other publications at the leading edge of new thinking and innovative practice on work, business, management, leadership, stewardship, career development, human resources, entrepreneurship, and global sustainability.

Since the company's founding in 1992, we have been committed to supporting the movement toward a more enlightened world of work by publishing books, periodicals, and other publications that help us to integrate our values with our work and work lives, and to create more humane and effective organizations.

We have chosen to focus on the areas of work, business, and organizations, because these are central elements in many people's lives today. Furthermore, the work world is going through tumultuous changes, from the decline of job security to the rise of new structures for organizing people and work. We believe that change is needed at all levels—individual, organizational, community, and global—and our publications address each of these levels.

We seek to create new lenses for understanding organizations, to legitimize topics that people care deeply about but that current business orthodoxy censors or considers secondary to bottom-line concerns, and to uncover new meaning, means, and ends for our work and work lives.

See next page for other products from Berrett-Koehler Publishers

Also available on audiotape

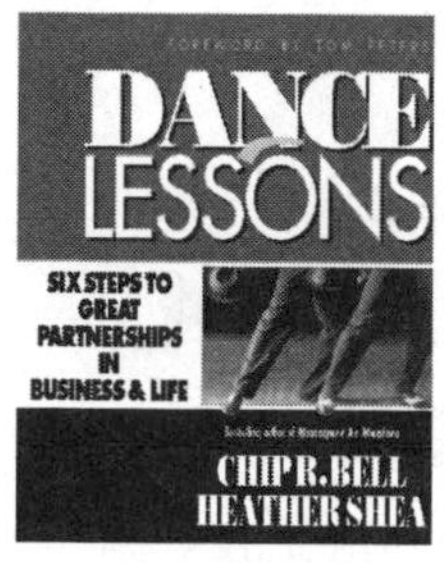

DANCE LESSONS AUDIO

THIS 3-HOUR, 2-cassette tape set features an abridged version of the book, read by Heather Shea.

2 cassettes, 3 hours, 10/98 • ISBN 1-56511-264-4
Item no. 12644-254 $17.95

Other leading-edge business books from Berrett-Koehler Publishers

CUSTOMERS AS PARTNERS

Building Relationships That Last

WRITTEN WITH PASSION and humor, this groundbreaking work provides step-by-step guidelines for enhancing long-term customer loyalty and achieving lasting success. Chip Bell offers insights on how to keep the quality of customer relationships central in every interaction by creating sustaining personal bonds-the true source of a company's profitability.

Paperback, 256 pages, 1/96 • ISBN 1-881052-78-8 CIP • **Item no. 52788-254 $15.95**
Hardcover 9/94 • ISBN 1-881052-54-0 CIP • **Item no. 52540-254 $24.95**

MANAGERS AS MENTORS

Building Partnerships for Learning

MANAGERS AS MENTORS is a provocative guide to helping associates grow and adapt in today's tumultuous organizations. Chip Bell persuasively shows that today, mentoring means valuing creativity over control, fostering growth by facilitating learning, and helping others get smart, not just get ahead. His hands-on, down-to-earth advice takes the mystery out of effective mentoring, teaching leaders to be the confident coaches integral to learning organizations.

Hardcover, 206 pages, 6/96 • ISBN 1-881052-92-3 CIP • **Item no. 52923-254 $24.95**

Available at your favorite bookstore, or call (800) 929-2929

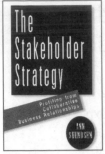

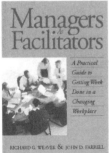

Put the leading-edge business practices you read about to use in your work and in your organization

Do ever you wish there was a forum in your organization for discussing the newest trends and ideas in the business world? Do you wish you could explore the leading-edge business practices you read about with others in your company? Do you wish you could set aside a few hours every month to connect with like-minded coworkers or to get to know others in your business community?

If you answered yes to any of these questions, then the answer is simple: Start a business book reading group in your organization or business community. For step-by-step advice on how to do just that, visit the Berrett-Koehler website at <www.bkpub.com> and click on "Reading Groups." There you'll find specific guidelines to help in all aspects of creating a successful reading group—from locating interested participants to selecting books and facilitating discussions.

These guidelines were created as part of the Business Literacy 2000 program launched by the Consortium for Business Literacy—a group of 19 business book publishers whose primary goal has been to promote the formation of business reading groups within corporations and business communities. Business Literacy 2000 is dedicated to providing you with tools to help you build a dialog with colleagues, share ideas, build lasting relationships, and bring new ideas and knowledge to bear in your work and organizations.

For more information on the Business Literacy 2000 program, guidelines for starting a business book reading group, or to browse or download the study guides that are available for our books, please visit our website at:

<www.bkpub.com>.

If you do not have Internet access, you may request information by contacting us at:

Berrett-Koehler Publishers
450 Sansome Street, Suite 1200
San Francisco, CA 94111
Tel: (415) 288-0260
Fax: (415) 362-2512
Email: bkpub@bkpub.com

Please be sure to include your name, address, phone number, and the information you would like to receive.